Tears

OF A FATHER

Tears OF A FATHER

My Story of Devastating Loss,
Tested Faith, and a Loving God

PAT SMITH

XULON PRESS

Xulon Press
2301 Lucien Way #415
Maitland, FL 32751
407.339.4217
www.xulonpress.com

Xulon
PRESS

Unless otherwise indicated, Scripture quotations taken from the New American Standard Bible (NASB). Copyright © 1960, 1962, 1963, 1968, 1971, 1972, 1973, 1975, 1977, 1995 by The Lockman Foundation. Used by permission. All rights reserved.

Scripture quotations taken from the English Standard Version (ESV). Copyright © 2001 by Crossway, a publishing ministry of Good News Publishers. Used by permission. All rights reserved.

Scripture quotations taken from the King James Version (KJV)–public domain.

Scripture quotations taken from the Holy Bible, New International Version (NIV). Copyright © 1973, 1978, 1984, 2011 by Biblica, Inc.™. Used by permission. All rights reserved.

Scripture quotations taken from the New King James Version (NKJV). Copyright © 1982 by Thomas Nelson, Inc. Used by permission. All rights reserved.

Printed in the United States of America.

ISBN-13: 978-1-6305-0600-1

In loving memory of my son, Grayson:

Although you are now with our Lord,
you will always be in the hearts and thoughts
of your family and many friends,
who love and miss you deeply.
You were taken from us much too soon,
but you are now happy and rejoicing
and in a far better place.
This we don't just hope to be true,
but know for an absolute fact—
and for that we are all truly thankful.
I look forward to the day when
we will be reunited in paradise.

And to my family:

I am truly blessed to have each one of you in my life.
I cannot imagine my life without each of you
being such a huge part of it.
I love all of you so very much.

Table of Contents

Introduction

Let's begin by getting my qualifications out of the way. I am not a psychiatrist. I am not a psychologist. Not a counselor of any kind. I have no college degrees that would make me qualified to help you deal with grief. I have no level of training whatsoever in how to deal with the loss of a loved one. In short, I have no qualifications to give advice on how to deal with the death of someone you love, except that I have experienced a loss so devastating I can't even begin to explain to you how hard it was and still is. The heartache I have endured has been excruciating and has felt unbearable at times. The pain seemed like it was never going to end. It still hurts so very much, but I have survived this horrific event. Survived and am getting stronger, thanks to the grace of God.

What I can tell you is my wife and I and our entire family would not have made it if not for our faith in God—faith that our God is a kind and caring God who would never leave us. No matter how hard life may get, no matter what tragedies may come our way, He will always be with us. Grief is very, very hard with God by your side. Without Him, it would almost be impossible to get through. I believe this to be an undeniable truth.

God watched over my family and me through the absolute darkest time of our lives. He brought us up from the depths of despair and has allowed us to emerge stronger Christians. We continue to hurt, and our lives will never be the same, but we are getting better thanks to our Lord and Savior.

This book reflects, in part, my feelings and experiences since the passing of my son, Grayson. Writing it has given me some peace as I continue to work through my loss. What you will find in its coming pages is my perspective on what you too may encounter as you work through the pain and grief associated with losing a loved one. I will also show you how my family and I navigated our way through the many difficult situations that we faced after losing Grayson. I will show you how desperately we needed God's healing hands on us during the days and months following Grayson's death and how God gave us hope when we thought all hope had forever been taken from our lives.

I lost my son. That is still so very hard for me to say and even harder for me to understand. Losing Grayson is absolutely the hardest experience that I have ever had to face. But I did face it, and if you are reading this book, you are probably facing a similar loss in your life. Even though my experience is about losing my son, I believe what I have written in this book is not specific to losing a child. I believe this book that God directed me to write can be helpful to anyone dealing with the loss of someone they love. I want so much for this book to help you in some way deal with your grief, and I want it to give you a view of dealing with loss from the perspective of someone who has experienced a life-changing loss of his own. I believe God uses people who are hurting to bring a message of hope to others. I feel He found someone in me who definitely fits that requirement.

It may not feel this way now, but I want you to know that you will make it through the pain you are currently experiencing. I know your heartache seems like it will never end, and you may feel as if God has abandoned you during the worst time of your life. I speak from experience when I tell you that your faith in God will be tested repeatedly as you struggle with the reality that someone you love so dearly will never be here on earth with you again. This realization is so very hard to grasp. The good news is, God will never leave you, no matter how many questions you throw at Him or how much you find yourself questioning your faith and questioning Him. He will always be there, walking right beside you, waiting and longing for you to turn to Him for comfort and wanting to ease your pain and heal your broken heart. I hope my book will help you to understand this, even as you continue to struggle to make it through one more day without someone you love so dearly—help you to realize that you need God now, more than ever, as you find yourself and your family hurting from this terrible loss. It is going to be a long and difficult journey, but with God by your side, you will once again find peace in your soul.

There is one additional detail that I feel is important for me to share with you. I want you to know that I am not an accomplished author publishing a second, third, or fourth book. I am a grieving parent trying my best to convey a message of hope to you and to others struggling with the pain and heartache of living through the loss of a loved one. This is the only book that I have ever attempted to write. I believe God directed me to put my story into print to help others who are suffering from a devastating loss of their own. He urged me to share my experiences with you as I journeyed through life after the death of my son. So as you read this book, read it as though you are listening to me tell my story. Because if I were to read it aloud right now, I believe it would sound just as if I were sitting with you in our living room sharing my heart. The only way I know how to write is by telling you about my experiences, about the way I felt at the different stages of my grief, and about how blessed I am to have a God who is healing my family and watching over my son until the day we are reunited with him in paradise.

Chapter 1

Making Sense of the Loss

❖

How do you make sense of the world when a loved one dies? I can tell you from my experience, you can't. It never makes sense. I have a wonderful family. We attend church regularly, we treat people with respect, and we always try to do what we feel is right. We are good people. Why would God allow Grayson, my twenty-six-year-old son, to be taken from me? I continually search for the answer, but still I don't know why something this devastating happened. The not knowing why has been one of the hardest things I have dealt with from day one. It still hurts so very much. Through countless sleepless nights and crying sessions, I can tell you I still have not figured it out. I will not fully know the answer to why this happened until I am also called to be with God and He tells me why this was in His plan—because I truly believe this was His plan.

My God is an omnipotent God. He knows all and has a plan for every one of us, even before we are born (Psalm 139:16). Who am I to question His plan? I will tell you who I am. I am a hurt and grieving parent struggling to survive the loss of my firstborn son whom I love with all my heart. I desperately need answers to so many questions, but the answers never seem to come.

I don't think my God is a God who would be angry with me for questioning why this happened. I believe He knows that in my grief I will have questions. Why Grayson? Why now? What did I do to deserve this happening to my family? Am I being punished for something I did? I think everyone who has experienced a loss has these or similar questions, and I think it is okay to raise these types of questions to God. I have talked with Him and prayed for answers so many times I cannot even begin to give you a number. It must be in the hundreds. I still do not have all of the answers that I'm seeking. I still don't think it's fair. But I know God is a merciful God and He has His reasons. He has an amazing plan of which this tragedy is a part. I have faith this is true.

I have come to accept the fact God does not owe me answers. No matter how much I want to believe He does, He doesn't. God's not providing me the answers to my questions has been extremely difficult for me to both understand and accept. Why would God not let me know why He allowed my son to die? It seems to me that if His plan contains something this devastating to my family and me He should have to explain His reasons. That seems only fair, right? After all, I am a faithful believer, one of His own. But I finally came to realize He doesn't owe me anything. Once I accepted that fact, I was able to move on, continue my grieving process, and begin to heal. God is a kind and caring God, and He does everything according to His plan. I don't know His plan and probably could not comprehend His plan if it were given to me. This is where my faith comes into play.

I have faith that God is in control and faith that He will guide me through this painful time in my life. I have faith God will use my loss for His good. It may be tomorrow, next week, or years from now, but I have faith that good will come from this loss. I have faith that my family and I will emerge stronger Christians and be better equipped to help others suffering from a loss. I have faith there is a reason for this tragedy and the pain it has brought into my life and the lives of my family members.

When I say there is a reason for this tragedy, I don't mean God caused Grayson to die. I serve a God who would never bring pain, grief, or heartache to anyone. God was not the source of the loss that devastated my family and me. It is always the devil who causes these types of horrific events to happen. He does this in an attempt to steal our joy, our hope, and our faith. I decided I was not going to allow the devil to win. I will not allow him to use the devastation that he caused in my life to separate me from my God.

Acknowledging that it was the devil behind my suffering was a major breakthrough for me. It helped me to begin thinking about the events of my life in the correct way. I don't blame God for all my pain and heartache. He was not the source of my sorrow. In fact, I believe that God hurts when I hurt and He cries when I cry. He agonizes when He sees you, me, or any of His children in pain. At least that is how it feels to me. He wants so much for my family and me to get through all our pain and sorrow and to experience happiness once again. I ask Him every day to help us to survive this devastating time in our lives. Because in our struggles we have God by our side, I am confident that my family will not only survive but we will become stronger, more committed Christians.

Through the grieving process, the lack of under-standing can take control of your life and consume you. It can hurt your relationship with God and your relationships with your family and friends. If this hap-pens, you will turn into a different person—one who is severely depressed, one who daily turns to alcohol or drugs to help cope with the loss. I can tell you from counseling and research, this is the rule and not the exception. I was determined not to let this type of destructive behavior take control of my life. You have the same choice. You can join the majority and turn to drugs and alcohol, or you can choose to believe God has a plan and that we don't have the capacity to understand His plan. For you to make the right choice, you must continue to have faith in Him.

Trusting God even when you don't understand His plan is the only way to get through the pain you are experiencing. Of course, saying it is one thing and doing it quite another. It has been extremely difficult for me to trust God during the devastation that has happened to my family. It will be hard for you too, but once you do, you will be amazed at how much better you feel and how your outlook on life will become so much brighter. The anger and torment you have been experiencing will suddenly be muted. My anger still is not and may never be gone completely, but when I trusted that the Lord was by my side and that He wanted to ease my pain, life became so much better.

This degree of trust and acceptance does not happen overnight; it takes some time and some real heart-to-heart talks with God. When you come to the point that you are able to believe He has a plan, trust in Him, and believe that this tragedy is a part of His plan, though, everything starts to get better. Your healing process starts in earnest at that point, at least mine did. I continue to improve most days, though I do experience occasional setbacks. I still have questions, get mad, and find myself falling back into depression at times, but the process has begun.

God is healing my family's pain and heartache, and He is guiding us through the worst time in our lives. I truly believe if God were not by our side, we could never make it through this pain and our lives would be changed for the worse. But God is there, easing our pain and helping us to get through our loss. He is fixing the brokenness of our lives and leading us forward. What an incredible healer He is. If you ask Him, He will help you too. You just need to ask.

Shortly after our tragedy, I had many conversations about Grayson with my friends and with a few of Grayson's closest friends. We talked about Grayson and his life, and the conversations often turned into discussions on why something this devastating had happened. In these discussions, I came up with several possible reasons why God had allowed Grayson to be taken from us at such a young age.

Like I said before, I still don't have all the answers as to why this horrible event happened and won't this side of heaven, but my mind kept searching for a reason. That was something I struggled with seemingly from the moment Grayson passed. For me, considering the possible positive explanations for our loss somehow made it easier to accept. Losing Grayson became ever so slightly less painful if I felt his death was for a higher purpose or for eliminating future pain and suffering.

In one instance, I was talking with one of Grayson's closest friends who was also having a very difficult time processing why this tragic event had happened. One possible scenario I discussed with him was that the devil was going to cause Grayson to be in a horrific accident the next morning and he would have suffered tremendously as a result. God knew this and called Grayson home early to save him from all the torment and agony the devil had planned for him. This seemed like something a kind and merciful God would do for one of His own, preventing pain and suffering. This possible reason really seemed to help Grayson's friend deal with the loss. It gave me some much-needed peace as well.

On another occasion, after discussing in much detail Grayson's life with a Christian friend, he presented me with another scenario, one that I probably would have never come up with on my own. Hearing it was a true blessing to me. It gave me peace when I thought about it accounting for my family's loss— so much peace that after I heard it I quit searching for other explanations. This one made so much sense to me there was no longer a reason to consider other possibilities.

Grayson had struggled with finding a way to work in the oil and gas industry, which was the field he dreamed of working in. He had worked in the oil business for several years and loved the work. Then a downturn in the industry left him unemployed. With so many people being laid off by oil companies, Grayson could not find another job in this field. He struggled for a while trying to find another career to pursue that he would love as much as oil and gas. He worked some odd jobs and continually prayed for guidance.

Shortly before his passing, Grayson's many prayers were answered and he was hired back into oil and gas work. He loved the new company and the people he was working with. He was doing tremendously well. He actually told me a week or so before he passed that he was happier than he had been in a long time. He was doing great at work, was making good money, had purchased a house, and was losing weight. To quote Grayson, life was good. Things were finally working out for him, and there was a lot of joy in his life. That is what really confused me. Why allow Grayson to go through all the trials and tribulations and then take him away just as he had turned things around and was doing so well? I couldn't figure out why a just and caring God would allow something that seemed so unfair to happen to him.

The answer to that question, given to me by my friend, was truly amazing. He summed the answer up in four powerful words: "God heard Grayson's prayers." These words didn't sound like the answer I was looking for. They didn't even make sense to me. But then he explained what he meant by his statement, and the explanation he gave to me made me stop and cry— tears of joy this time rather than of pain. What he told me gave me more hope and peace than any words anyone else had spoken to me. He said, in summary, God told Grayson what he needed to do to turn his life around and to be able to do the things he desired most. Grayson listened and did the things God instructed him to do. In following God's directions, life started getting better for Grayson. As he continued along this path, his everyday life steadily improved and his happiness continued to grow. And then, when Grayson finally reached the place where he had hoped to be, God said, "Well done, My son. Today you will be with Me in paradise."

Just think, Grayson did what God directed him to do, and he received the best reward imaginable: he was called home to live with Christ in paradise! Does it get any better than that? This possible reason for Grayson's death gives me tremendous comfort. Again, this is only a guess. I will not know why this happened until I am in heaven, and at that point I probably won't care about having the why question answered. But this possible scenario gave me tremendous peace at a time when I was really struggling.

You and your family will also have to deal with why your loved one was taken from you. It is so very difficult not knowing why something this devastating happened to you. It can eat away at your soul if you let it. You must realize that it is the devil at work and that he is the source of your pain and suffering. Knowing the source of your loss helps. It still doesn't answer the question of why this was a part of God's plan, but as I said, God does not owe us an answer. Once you come to terms with and are able to accept that statement, you will begin to move forward with your healing process. Don't let the not knowing why tear you and your family apart. Don't let your unanswered questions consume the remainder of your life. You must have faith that God has a reason for this tragedy and accept that you may never know what that reason is. Know too that God feels your pain and He wants to take away the hurt you are currently experiencing. He is a kind and caring God who wants to give you peace and comfort as you struggle with your loss. It will take some time, but He will bring you and your family the peace you so desperately need.

Going through our first Christmas without Grayson was very, very difficult for my family. I talked to God even more during that holiday season. In my many talks with God, I realized something awesome. It was something I had known for most of my life, but it was just now becoming clear in my mind. I realized God had sent His Son to die for you and for me. He sacrificed His Son for our sins.

Pause for a moment. Let that sink in. He sacrificed His Son for us. What an incredible price for God to willingly pay, all because we are sinners.

Not until my own loss did I really understand the tremendous sacrifice God willingly made for each of us. It had to be excruciatingly hard for Him to send His Son, His only Son, to be abused, tortured, and put to death for our sins. It shows how much He loves and truly cares for us. This is the greatest sacrifice anyone could possibly make. Choosing to give up your life would be an incredibly difficult decision, but giving your only child up to be tortured and crucified? That is true sacrifice.

Considering this helped me see that God was not having me go through anything He Himself had not already experienced in an even more devastating way. He knows my pain, and He understands my suffering. He wants to bring me comfort and peace. The healing process has begun, and I trust He will continue to care for my family and me until we once again experience His peace in our lives.

We sang a song in church that same Christmas. The song seemed to speak to me in a very personal way. The words of the song seemed like they were speaking directly to me and giving me hope and direction as I continued to struggle with why Grayson had been taken from me. After listening to the song, I became so emotional that I didn't know if I was going to make it out of church. The words meant so much to me that their message caused me to break down and cry. It was a Life Church original song called "With Us." Some of the lyrics in this song that really spoke to me are, "When we don't understand, we know You're working for our good...We're trusting in Your plan, Your purpose always wins...In every moment You are with us."[1] These words—powerful words made even more powerful when put to music—cut straight to my heart. I encourage each of you to download this song, listen to its message, and believe. We must all trust that the Lord has a plan. Trust, like the words of the song

---

[1] Life.Church Worship, *With Us* (2016), https://open.life.church/resources/2912-with-us

set out, that even when we don't understand, He is working for our good.

So no, I don't understand why I lost Grayson, but having the faith to know this is God's plan and He is working for our good has helped me tremendously as I navigate through this chapter of my life. I know God's plan will include good emerging from this tragedy. Knowing that has given my family and me peace and hope for the future. Keep your faith strong, and He will bring you comfort too. He truly is with us.

Chapter 2

Life Is a Journey

❖

Recently, my church had a series of lessons about our "life journey". These sermons spoke to me in my state of confusion and depression, at a time when I really needed some understanding. We have all experienced many peaks and valleys in our lives, good times and bad. When life is great and everything is going smoothly, I am on a mountaintop. It is easy then for me to trust God, to thank Him, and to praise His name. However, when Grayson was suddenly taken from me and I found myself hurting and grieving in a deep, deep valley, thanking Him and praising His name was so much harder. Harder? Try nearly impossible. How could I possibly praise His name and trust Him when He had just allowed someone I love so dearly to be taken from me? Regaining my trust in God was something I so desperately needed to do before continuing my walk through this terrible valley. I truly needed something to hold on to as I continued to hit new lows in my life. What I needed was a God I could trust and believe in—my God.

But where was my God during this low time in my life? Where was He when I lost Grayson and felt darkness and hopelessness all around me? Where was He when I was feeling so lost and confused? Where is He now while I am attempting to cope with all the pain and misery in my life and in the lives of my family members? He was, He is, and He will always be beside me, walking right next to me as I journey through life.

If I truly have faith in God, then I must have faith in Him and praise Him in all things, always. Not just when things are going great, but when things are bad, even very bad. What an incredibly hard concept to grasp. But I can't pick and choose when I will and when I will not praise God. If I am truly a Christian, I must constantly praise God, through all of the many peaks and valleys of my life journey. I must trust in Him, have faith in Him, and know that He is walking with me as I journey through this low point in my life. I must trust that He is with me when I am on mountaintops and that He is pulling me even closer as I travel through the valleys of my life. In the low times, when the days seem to take more than I can possibly give, I feel my Father's loving arms around me, holding me up, giving me strength and leading me forward. He comforts and protects me as I continue the most difficult walk of my life through this valley.

From my standpoint, not too long ago, I was on top of a mountain. I was an officer of a Fortune 500 company. I had been with this company for over fifteen years and truly believed I would retire there. I was so confident, in fact, that I accepted a transfer to move to a neighboring state when the office in my home state closed. Except for my living away from home four and a half days a week, my family was doing very well. Everyone was healthy, happy and moving ahead with his or her life plans. My wife Kathy and I were experiencing the joy of spending time with our first grandson. Life was good. I thanked God often for the blessings He had given to my family and me.

But then a year ago my journey took me from the mountaintop to a deep, deep valley. Grayson died suddenly, and I quit my job so I could be home with my family to try to help them work through this painful time in their lives. It is hard to believe such a horrible change of circumstances could happen in a matter of a few of days, but it did. Everything is different now; nothing will ever be the same. I am back home with no job, hurting from the loss of my firstborn son. I am trying to help my family get through this devastating loss. Trying to lead them through this low point in their lives. Trying just to survive! What a terrible change in our lives. In the blink of an eye, my family's everyday lives changed for the worse. I never thought anything like this could ever happen to me, but it did.

Again, it is so easy to praise God when life is good and so much harder to do when bad things are happening in your life. I couldn't fathom praising God for my new life. It seemed like an impossible thing to do. And it was. But until I did, I was not going to get better, and until I got better I could not help my family move through their grieving processes. Praising God for allowing Grayson to enter paradise—what an unthinkable, bizarre thing for me to do. But think about it: he is in paradise. There is no better place for him to be, and there is no better person to be watching over him than our Lord. When you think about it in those terms, it is much easier to be thankful. Easier, but still an incredibly difficult thing to do.

My family and I have discussed Grayson's being in paradise on several occasions. The time I remember with the most clarity was on Grayson's birthday, four months after his death. As we talked with each other and with a few of our friends, the common theme was that Grayson was having the best birthday he had ever experienced. He was having his first birthday celebration in heaven. Wow!, What a birthday it must have been! I remember picturing in my mind Grayson's smiling face. That seemed to make the reality that I wasn't celebrating his birthday with him for the first time in twenty-seven years a little more bearable. I still miss him so much. But I know he is happy and rejoicing in heaven, and that is what matters most to me.

From this standpoint, I think of myself as being selfish when I grieve. I know Grayson is in a much better place and would not come back for anything. I know he is living in paradise with no pain of any kind, and he is feeling no anxiety or stress. He is so happy to be at home with his heavenly Father. However, his earthly father still misses him so very much. Is this a selfish thing? Maybe. But even if so, my family and I will continue to be selfish because we will never stop missing Grayson, ever. He will always be close to our hearts and be a part of our family.

In spite of my grief, though, I have come to the place where I am so thankful for God's bringing Grayson home to live with Him. Once I reached that point, my everyday life started to improve. Things got better. Slowly, but they did start to get better.

I continue to talk with God daily, and He continues to help me through my grieving process. He also continues to direct me on how to help my family through their struggles. Talking with God and trusting He will help you through this challenging time in your life is the best advice I can give to you or to anyone grieving from a loss. It is hard, but until you do, you will not get better. And until you are better, it is extremely difficult to help others work through their own struggles with the loss.

One good thing that can come from the low points in your life journey, the times when you find yourself traveling through a very deep and dark valley, is the opportunity to strengthen your personal relationship with God. I know over the past year my family has prayed more and read the Bible more than at any other point in our lives. We make our hearts known to God several times a day, every day.

If you don't remember anything else I have written in this book, please remember this: this is the time, in your grief, to get up close and personal with God. I have, and He listens to me and gives me comfort when I think I will never have comfort again. The Bible teaches His name is Immanuel, which means "God with us." That means He is *always* with us. So, in the valleys of your journey through life, talk with Him and be comforted by Him. This is what I needed and what I believe everyone needs when hurting from a loss. Draw close to Him, and He will comfort you.

I have never been closer to our Lord than I am at this very moment. I hope in my daily walk through life people will see something different in me. I pray they will see a strong man of faith who battled through a tragedy and emerged a stronger, more committed Christian. That is how I feel, and I hope it is evident to all who meet me.

Being closer and more intimate with God has meant that I talk to Him daily about my struggles. He answers my prayers and gives me direction for my life in many different ways. Sometimes it is a call or a text from a friend just when I need it. Sometimes it is at church in the pastor's message or in the words of a worship song. Other times, it is just seeing the loving and trusting eyes of my three-year-old grandson that gives me peace and lets me know I am going to be all right. I give praise to God for the answers He has given to me through so many different avenues. The key is just keeping my eyes and ears open for the answers, from wherever they may come.

I often find myself crying in church as I focus on the words of the worship songs. Almost every week at least one song speaks to me and gives me comfort, direction, or the answers to one of my many prayers. Try really concentrating on the words to the worship songs you hear. Don't just sing them; hear them and receive their message to you. It is truly amazing what you can hear if you listen closely.

What I hear moves me to tears constantly, and those tears seem to wash away some of my pain. I recently read a poster that sums this point up for me.

It read, "When you're happy, you enjoy the music. When you're sad, you understand the lyrics." Boy do I understand the lyrics! I pray listening to the lyrics and understanding the message will likewise give you some peace in your heart and answers to the many questions you are desperately searching for as you continue your journey.

My family's journey out of this valley has been a slow climb with many hardships experienced by each of us along the way. We must navigate our way through the many obstacles that we face as we continue our journey out of this valley. But my God is the best guide we could possibly have as we start our ascent. I trust the Lord will lead my family and me out of this valley soon. I feel and pray we have hit rock bottom and are now turning the corner and moving ahead in our journey. We will once again move forward and upward to new mountaintops, or at least for now, the top of a hill. God has a plan to get us out of this valley. I know He does, and I know we will.

Everyone says life is short. Whether you live to be six or one hundred and six, it is a brief period of time compared to eternity. The way I look at it, no matter how long I live, it will be like one or two seconds compared to eternity. Even though Grayson is not physically here with me now, I will be able to spend most of my time with him. The few seconds of eternity during which I will be without him will be difficult but will pass quickly. Our family will be reunited in paradise. Talk about something great to look forward to! We will live together in paradise for eternity! It's hard to think of anything better than that. I know Grayson will be waiting there to greet us all with huge hugs and his patented smile. I can hardly wait for him to show us around.

Chapter 3

Finding Your "New Normal"

❖

During my grieving process, someone told me I needed to find my "new normal." Some books I subsequently read also talked about that same subject. What does that mean—a new normal? The way it was explained to me, my new normal is how my life is right now and how it will continue to be, without Grayson's physically being a part of it. After over a year, my family and I are still trying to figure out what our new normal is. We will never have our old normal lives back, so we must determine what our new normal is and begin living it. This single act is one of the hardest things that my family and I have ever attempted to do, but it is something that we must do in order to continue our healing process.

Our new normal will be without Grayson's presence, so it cannot be better; it will just be different. Grayson will always be with us in spirit. We will never forget him and how he touched, and continues to touch, our lives every day. I can still see his smile and hear his laugh, and I am sure this will not change for the rest of my life. But my family and I need to get to a place where we feel our lives are moving forward, our new normal.

When I talk about a new normal, I am reminded of something written in one of the many books I have read. It is a story that describes the way the author feels about his loss. His story explains his new normal life in terms that, for me, are easy to understand. It explains exactly how I feel about my new normal life. I don't remember exactly how it goes, but I will apply the author's illustration to my personal loss to convey his message.

Losing Grayson was like being in a devastating accident that caused me to painfully and tragically lose my arm. It was a horrific shock to have my arm forever taken from me. It is so very difficult for me, my family, and my friends to understand why something this tragic had to happen. I go through all the stages of grief. I don't believe this really happened; this is not real. I am bitterly angry this has happened to me and angry at the effect it has had and will continually have on my family. The agony that I experience from my loss seems to attack every aspect of my life. I find it very difficult to function every day in a way that even resembles a normal life. I can't imagine having to live the remainder of my life this way, without my arm. My life, and the lives of my family members, will never be the same because of this terrible tragedy. My life as I have always known it will be so very different as I attempt to move forward without my arm.

After a prolonged period of being angry about my loss, I become very dejected because I finally come to grips with the fact that I will never again have my arm with me. Depression sets in as I realize the finality of what has happened. And I begin to question God a lot. Why did He allow this to happen? What did I do to deserve this? Why me? (Do these emotions and questions sound familiar?)

Then, after having run through all the grief stages, I finally decide I must accept what has happened and move ahead, start living my life again without my arm. I come to grips with the fact that nothing I do will allow me to regain what I have lost. I owe it to my family to accept that fact, to have a positive attitude, and to begin moving forward with my life. I must be the best person I can be while I bear this devastating loss.

So, I move on with my life, but it is a very different life from my normal life before the tragedy. There is a part of me missing, a part that I cannot replace with any of the other parts of my body, no matter how hard I try, and this brings new limitations and forces me to find new ways of navigating my world. I will always remember when I had my arm, and I will always miss having it with me. I now feel incomplete and inadequate because a huge part of my life has forever been taken from me. But this is how my life will be from this day forward; this is my new normal.

I could not have come up with a better illustration for the way I feel about my new life without Grayson. This analogy meant a lot to me while I was trying to find and understand my new normal life, and it has also helped me to explain the concept to well-wishing people who have not experienced a life-changing loss of their own. Comparing losing Grayson to losing my arm gives others a sense of the continuing loss I will deal with for the remainder of my life. It gives them a glimpse of the pain I continually feel. Everyone can imagine the tremendous pain and suffering they would endure if they were to suddenly and unexpectedly have their arm ripped from their body. Multiply the agonizing pain of losing an arm by 10,000 and you will not even be close to the pain I feel every day from losing my son. Thinking about losing a limb helps others to understand the immense pain I have in my life right now and how different the remainder of my life will be moving forward without my firstborn son.

My new normal life will always have a void that cannot be filled. I need to move forward with my life, but Grayson will always be a missing part of it, and in his place will be an emptiness, a hole in my heart. Just like the example of losing my arm, Grayson was a part of my life I was used to having with me, but moving forward, he won't be there. I will carry this loss with me until the day I am called home to be with my heavenly Father. Only then will I be able to stop grieving the loss of my son.

It is so very hard for me to come to grips with the fact that Grayson will never be here on earth with me again. It seems unreal to have to live my life without my oldest child. It still feels like a bad dream from which I will never awaken. But, for my family and myself, I must accept the reality that he is gone. I must move forward and start living my new normal life without Grayson. We must all determine what our new normal life is so we can move forward and live out the life God has planned for each of us—a very different life than the one that we thought we would have, to be sure.

God is helping me through my loss and directing me toward my new normal. It is not drugs, alcohol, or locking myself away from everyone that helps me to find my new normal and move forward with my life. No, those things only dull the pain and postpone the healing process. Only God can get me through the agonizing pain that now fills every day of my life. Only God can repair my heart that has been broken into so many small pieces. Only God can bring me the peace I need as I continue to try so hard to find and understand my new normal life. I need Him so much right now.

Prior to trusting God and asking Him to guide me through my grief, I was not getting better. I continually felt hurt, confused, and depressed. My life was filled with sadness and so much pain. Once I put my trust in Him, though, my healing process began and I finally started to feel some peace in my soul. This peace has given me the ability to lead my family through this horrible time in their lives, which is the most important responsibility I have. I pray every day for God to grant me the wisdom and ability to help bring my family through the grieving process and help them find their new normal. There is no way I could do this without Him.

That's not to say there isn't a time to focus on loss. In the beginning, it consumed my every thought and action. I felt broken, confused, and betrayed and experienced a pain I thought would never leave me. This is normal. Everyone enduring a loss will experience the different stages of the grieving process (denial, anger, bargaining, depression, and acceptance). Reflecting back, I went through some of the stages multiple times. Working my way through these stages was a normal and necessary part of my healing process.

In my grief, I hit lows I never imagined I would ever experience. There were definitely times when I didn't know if I would make it. But I *had* to make it. I had to make it for my family. So, after many weeks of tremendous suffering, I decided I needed to pick myself up and move on with my life. If my only focus continued to be on my loss and the immense pain I was feeling, my future life would be full of heartache and depression. That was not the life I desired for myself or for my family. That was also not what God wanted for me. It's not what He wants for any of us.

God helped me to begin to concentrate on the good in my life. The blessings God has given to me are many. And when I began focusing on the many blessing that remain in my life, I was wonderfully surprised at how incredibly blessed my life truly is. I have an unbelievable wife, two children I love dearly and am extremely proud of, a daughter-in-law who is wonderful, and a grandson who brightens up a room simply by walking into it. I have loving parents, brothers, and sisters. Except for my recent loss, I have a life most would consider outstanding. Focusing on the good remaining in my life has helped me work through my grief and begin to move forward. I have begun to find my new normal life. It is a very different life, certainly, but one that can still be great despite my loss, with much peace, joy, and hope.

You must find your new normal life too. It will take some time, and it will not be easy, but it is something everyone dealing with a loss must eventually come to grips with. Your life is not over, although I can say from experience that there are many times when it does feel that way. God has planned a future and a purpose for the remainder of your life. You must determine what the future holds for you and begin living your new normal life. It is not the life you planned and definitely not the one you had hoped for, but with God by your side, it can still be a life with meaning and purpose. It is so very difficult, but you must find your new normal as soon as you are able.

Chapter 4

Life Goes On

❖

I struggled with including this chapter. It is the last one I wrote. I inserted it into this book and removed it on several occasions. When I read all the other chapters, they seemed more positive and uplifting. This chapter, though I thought it necessary, seemed to not have the same positive vibe as the other chapters. However, I finally decided to include it because I think it is important for you to know certain things you can expect as you move forward. I believe this chapter will help you to see that people are basically kind and well-meaning, even if it may not seem that way to you when you are grieving. Additionally, it will demonstrate events that, absent my loss, would have seemed a part of normal everyday life but were instead extremely painful experiences I had to deal with as my life moved forward. In a nutshell, everything I experience makes me think of Grayson, and this causes me to look at certain events in my life differently.

We have just come off the topic of finding your new normal, and along those lines, I want to prepare you for a hard truth. While you are working through your grief and attempting to find your new normal, everyone else will have already resumed their lives. We have good friends who care deeply for us, but after a brief time, they went back to living their normal lives. We still desperately needed their support, but they all had jobs, children, aging parents, and other responsibilities that once again filled their days. They aren't bad or insensitive people; they were just getting back to living their everyday lives. Life went on and is now back to normal, for them.

The few days between Grayson's death and his funeral, we had many friends visiting us, checking on us, and trying their best to take care of us while we were suffering through our loss. They brought us food and drinks, and they were good to come by often and talk with us. We heard wonderful stories about Grayson, and we recalled some of the fun times we had with him. It was good remembering Grayson with our friends. It gave us some joy in a time when we desperately needed it.

But a couple of weeks after the funeral, nearly all our friends had returned to their busy schedules. They stopped calling and checking on us. We never saw them except accidentally at some random place like the store or the bank. It was as if everyone thought that since it had been a few weeks we should be over our grieving and be back to normal. I wish they knew just how far from being back to normal we actually were. We continued to hurt and struggle, but most of our friends just did not understand how much pain remained in our lives.

During the week leading up to the funeral, I saw a number of old friends I had not seen since Grayson was in high school. Their sons and Grayson had played high school sports together. It was so good to see them and be able to talk with them about the good old days of watching our boys play ball and traveling together to different sports venues. Talking about some of the specific games and seasons gave me a few minutes of joy in the midst of all my suffering. It was really good for me to reminisce with my old friends. They stopped by a couple of times and said we needed to get together for lunch or dinner, and then they were off. I never heard from them again. It would have been so great to eat lunch and talk about happier times with them, but they never called. If they had only realized how much a lunch or two would have meant to me I'm sure they would have made it a point to call. But they went back to their normal lives again, while I sat at home longing for some type of normalcy in my life.

Grayson's passing reunited me with a large number of my work colleagues too. Many had traveled up from Texas to attend the funeral. It was so thoughtful of them to make that trip. However, that was the last time I saw or heard from most of them. I received a few texts from a couple of the guys, asking how I was doing, but most went back to their day-to-day lives immediately, and I have not heard from them since. It made me sad at first, but I know we are still friends, and if I ever go back to Fort Worth, they will all want to meet up with me after work and get caught up on what's happening in all of our lives. They just didn't have any idea how badly I needed to hear from my friends.

If this isn't clear, let me say I am not casting blame or pointing fingers at anyone. If I had not gone through this experience myself, I probably would have behaved in much the same way toward someone in my shoes. My point is, not everyone experienced the magnitude of loss my family and I experienced. Our friends' lives pretty much went back to normal even though ours didn't.

Not only is my life not going back to normal, but I also now seem to be viewing life events with a Grayson slant. What I mean is, I imagine in certain moments how I would be experiencing them with Grayson if he were physically there with me. It can be quite overwhelming, but I think it is normal for my mind to function this way. I want to prepare you for this and let you know it is probably going to happen to you too. The Grayson slant is not limited to me; my whole family experienced the same type of emotional experiences as life moved on for our friends. I will give you a few examples of how normally happy life events took sad turns for us while those around us were unaware of our pain.

About nine months after the funeral, Kathy, my daughter Caroline, and I attended a gender reveal party for a family with whom we are very close. It was a lovely party where we were able to see many of our good friends. Kathy helped with refreshments, and we were all very excited for the couple. Everyone was wishing them the best as they approached the birth of their first child, and they were so appreciative to everyone who came to celebrate their good fortune. What an exciting time in their lives. It was a great celebration. Life was good.

Then, the very next day, Kathy co-hosted an engagement shower for a young man named John (to whom you will be introduced in the next chapter) and his bride-to-be. She had worked on the decorations and some of the food for the occasion. This was a no-men-allowed, women-only shower, so Kathy and Caroline attended without me. When they returned home, they told me all about how great of an event it was. Everyone was so happy for the couple as they prepared to start a life together, and the couple was happy and appreciative for the celebration, the gifts, and all the well wishes that they had received. Again, life was good.

Then things took a very bad turn. We struggled for much of the next week, Kathy much more so than I. You see, even though we were very happy for both these young families, we began to think about Grayson. We would never be able to see him find the love of his life and get married. We would not get to see his smiling face after he witnessed the birth of his firstborn child. We would never get to spoil and play with the grandchildren he would have provided us. Austin and Caroline's children would never know their Uncle Grayson and would not get to grow up playing with his children. We were filled with sadness because Grayson never experienced these happy times in his life. This was a sadness we had experienced shortly after Grayson's death, and we now were experiencing it all over again. Pain of this kind is unbearable. It is a gut-wrenching pain that you cannot possibly understand until you have lived through it and one that you do not recover from quickly. The pain from the thoughts of what could have been for Grayson lingered for an extended period of time. Even though these were happy events, the Grayson slant overwhelmed us with so much sorrow.

Another instance of my Grayson slant came in my work setting, about eight or nine months after the funeral. I had started working with a few people I had never met before in an attempt to form a new company, and my office was next to the office of a strong Christian named Ross. Even though we had just met, Ross ministered to me and helped me through many of the trials I was experiencing from the loss of Grayson. He is a very good man whom Kathy and I believe God put into my life to comfort me and give me strength when I needed it most.

Even so, Ross has a son. And at the time, Ross's son had an office in the same building as our new company. A few times a week, he would walk over to his dad's office to talk about his son's latest baseball game. The doors were open and the walls were very thin, so I could usually hear most of their conversations. They would talk about how his son, Ross's grandson, batted and fielded in the game or tournament he had played in the previous weekend. They talked about all the plays he had made and his reaction after the win or loss. It was just good, normal, everyday talk between a father and son.

I loved and hated hearing the stories they shared. It was good to hear Ross being told about his grandson's baseball performances and his son's coaching strategies, to hear a family sharing life's fun times with each other. However, it was also very difficult for me to hear these stories. Grayson played baseball and basketball in high school. I know he would have coached his son, and he would have loved sharing stories with me about the games I missed and rehashing the best moments from the games I was able to attend—which I assure you would have been most.

Sometimes I smiled at the conversations between Ross and his son because I put myself and Grayson in their shoes. I believe our conversations would have been very similar. Other times, their stories had the complete opposite effect on me. On these harder occasions, I would just close my door and cry for a while because I knew Grayson and I would never be able to have those talks. It is very hard on me knowing that I will never be able to share those good stories with him. I will never hear how my grandson batted so well or how he ran the wrong way down the base path. These are things that I was so looking forward to experiencing with Grayson, but those talks will never happen. Not having the future with Grayson that I always thought I would have is a hurt which I will continue to experience for the rest of my life.

Thankfully, I do have my grandson Callum, who at age three, is already playing sports. I talk to my son Austin about his practices and his improvement. I can't wait to watch Cal play and share these good times with Austin. It makes me smile when I think about the joy we will experience and the good times we will have watching Cal play ball. I know Grayson will also be smiling as he watches and roots him on. I just know he will.

These are just a few examples of how losing a loved one changes how you view different events in your life and how grief continues longer than most people around you realize. Normally happy events—and events that have you feeling genuinely happy again initially—will cause you so much pain. The pain is unintentional, as others will not feel your sorrow or consider the pain an event may cause you. You may think them insensitive, but they are not. They are just living their normal lives. They mean well, but they just don't understand your pain and don't realize how much you truly need them beyond the initial weeks after your loss.

I want you to know when this becomes your experience, if it has not already, that what you are feeling is normal. It is normal to wonder why your friends have forgotten about you. It is normal to be sad about otherwise happy events. It is normal for others to think you should be back to normal when in reality you will continue to hurt for the rest of your life. These things are not specific to you; they are struggles we all experience. They are part of the grieving process that everyone who experiences a loss must navigate their way through.

It will be easy to hold grudges over these types of behaviors, but don't. Grudges and hard feelings just hamper the healing process. They will add to your struggles rather than help you through them. Internally, and externally if appropriate, forgive everyone who unintentionally causes you pain. They don't mean to hurt you; they just don't know what to say or how to act. If you have never experienced it yourself, it's hard to know how to help someone who is grieving the loss of a loved one.

When you find yourself emotional and depressed because you have slanted a life event toward the one you lost, focus on the positive. That's what I try to do. Focus on the good coming from these events and be happy for those involved. Life goes on for them, which is a good thing. It's hard, but keeping a positive attitude is what can help get you through this terrible time in your life. For me, it is the only thing that helps lessen the pain that comes from the Grayson slant I experience on so many occasions.

And whatever you do, don't avoid happy occasions. You need to stay connected with your friends and attend normal life events, no matter how much it may hurt later. In spite of our pain, it has been important to my family to support our friends and let them know we still care. I was so proud of Kathy for taking part in both of the activities I mentioned. She is an amazing person. I want to point out that we were not sad at these events; we became sad after we got home and began to reflect. I believe it is good for us to continue to get out and participate in these types of celebrations. At this point in our lives, I don't think we can attend enough happy events. It is a part of our healing process. Even though each may give us some unintended pain, they also help us to smile for a while and reconnect with our friends.

To this point in the chapter, I have set out how people's lives very quickly go back to normal and shared with you examples of how most of our friends went back to living their day-to-day lives without much thought of our struggles. I have also attempted to show you how loss slants your view of some of life's normal, happy events and how it can produce sorrow and depression from them. The pain you will feel from these types of occasions is real, and I thought that I needed to prepare you for it. Now, I would like to tell you about exceptions to what I have written in this chapter. God is good, and He placed a few special people in our path to help us through this painful time in our lives.

Even though I am appreciative of all the people who checked on my family and cared for us after our loss, there are two people who have stayed with us for a year and counting—two amazing people I truly believe God sent to Kathy and me to help us in our time of need.

I have a good friend living in Nevada named Keith who tries to call or text me every week to see how I am doing. This means the world to me. When I see his name show up on my phone, I smile because I know I am about to have a good talk with a great friend. We not only talk about my loss, my life, and God, but we also talk about other things, like what bad golfers we are. The last time he came to town, we played a couple rounds of really bad golf, which was really great. At night, we sat on the back porch and just talked. We did that for a couple nights in a row. That was so healing for me. We are making plans to get together again later this summer. Keith has helped me so much over the past year. I don't know why he felt the need to stay in touch with me when most of my friends who live much closer did not, but I know God had a hand in it, and I thank Him for that daily.

As for Kathy, she has a few friends who live close to us who check on her periodically. A couple of her girl-friends will occasionally invite her to go out to lunch or to go shopping. She is always grateful to get out of the house and spend time with them. One friend in particular named Kerri has helped Kathy find some peace in her life just by being there for her and by letting her know that she truly cares about her. Kerri is a very strong Christian who has been able to talk to Kathy from the standpoint of someone who has also experienced the loss of a loved one, having lost her sister. She has no idea how much she has helped Kathy, both mentally and spiritually. I am sure Kathy's struggles would have been even more intense if not for Kerri's taking the time to be there for her, comforting her in her time of need.

There were also those who didn't hang around as long as Keith and Kerri but who walked quite a few miles with us through our grief. A couple of Grayson's friends stayed in touch with us for a few months. They told us tremendous stories of Grayson and their friendship with him. Grayson, they said, had been a great friend to them, and they all agreed that if Grayson was your friend, he was your friend for life. They loved him so very much. These stories were and continue to be a blessing to us.

Over the holidays and on Grayson's birthday, we received many calls and texts from our close friends and from some of Grayson's closest friends. These small acts of kindness meant so much to us as we continued to struggle with our loss. To know someone was thinking of our family and our struggles during these extremely challenging times helped us to heal. Even though their lives went back to normal, these few friends made the extra effort to reach out to us and to let us know that we were in their thoughts. What an incredible blessing this was to my family.

While it may often feel like you are alone and the only one who sees your pain, I bet if you look at your life, you can identify a Keith, a Kerri, or a small group of people who try their best to anticipate the days that will be hardest for you, like holidays, and reach out to you. They let you know that you are not alone. These friends and others who check on us for an extended length of time probably don't realize how important what they do for us actually is. It is so important to have people in our lives who continue to be there for us. Without them, the healing process would take much, much longer and our pain would be even more intense.

I am so thankful for everyone who cared for my family, but I am especially thankful for the handful of friends who stayed in contact with us and continued to check on us for months after our loss. Like everyone else, their lives went back to normal, but they made the extra effort to stay in touch with us to make sure we were okay. Their continued support helped Kathy and me so much in our time of grief. I pray Kathy and I will be friends like Kerri and Keith to our friends, should the need arise.

I am not bitter toward my friends who did not continue their support of my family. I don't harbor bad feelings toward anyone who did not check on me or stay in touch with me after that first horrible month. Yes, for a while Kathy and I felt hurt. We had thought we had better friends who would continue to check on us through our sorrow. However, being mad and resenting people for getting back to living their lives is pointless. Nothing good can come from it. We don't know what others were experiencing in their own lives during our time of grieving. They may have had their own struggles of which we were not aware.

I choose to be very grateful for those who have stuck with us for so many months rather than disappointed in those who have not. Staying positive has helped me to not be bitter and to maintain my friend-ships. I know that before I experienced a loss of my own, I probably wouldn't have thought to stay in touch for months with friends experiencing their own life-changing losses. That seems like a no-brainer now, but not before. Focus on the positive, the friends who con-tinue to check on you. They are truly blessings from God. The ones who don't check on you are still good friends; they just don't know what to do or how badly you need them.

I now know if a tragedy should befall a friend of mine, I need to stay in contact with them for much longer than I would have thought necessary. Keeping in touch with and continuing to check on your grieving friends and their families is the most important task there is. Grieving people need friends with them for much longer than a week or two. Having gone through my loss and my grieving process will help me to be more sensitive to those God brings into my life who are suffering. I believe this is a very good perspective that comes from a loss. We must be comforters and provide emotional support over a longer period whenever the opportunity arises.

Yes, as the title of this chapter states, life goes on. But we, as Christians, must make sure we min-ister to and comfort those going through loss as our lives go back to normal. They need us more than ever during this time in their lives. Since we have had similar experiences, we know what they need and we know many of the struggles they will face. We need to be there for them in their time of need and make sure that they know God loves them. We know their pain, and we know their grief will not go away in a few weeks. They need to know we are there for them and that they can count on us supporting them for as long as it takes. Leaning on the Lord for strength and comfort and having friends like us continually checking on them is what they desperately need when they are suffering. From our experience with loss, we know this to be true.

Chapter 5

Last Words Are Important

❖

About eight years before Grayson's death, God welcomed into paradise another very special person who was very close to our family. Sherri's death was sudden and unexpected. At her funeral, my family and I heard a moving message from her son, John. John's testimonial was so powerful and had such a huge, lasting impact on my family that we felt the need to share his words of wisdom with the congregation at Grayson's funeral. (We also felt that this was something Grayson would have wanted us to share.) I will to try to convey John's message to you because if it has the same effect on you that it has had on my family and me, it will be a blessing that you and your family could potentially receive multiple times a day. If you take to heart what this brave young man shared with us that day, you will find it truly amazing. It is amazing because it is not a one-time activity but a change in your way of life. In effort you put forth, it's a minor change to your daily activities, but in meaning for your life, it has huge, huge ramifications. You will see what I mean as you read on.

To give you some backstory, my family had a very close relationship with Sherri's family. They were like our extended family. Our kids played together, participated in dance together, and played on the same sports teams, which Sherri's husband and I coached together when the kids were young. Our families went out to eat together, attended church together, and even vacationed together. Their children were like our children and vice versa. We were about as close as two families could be. Life was good.

Then tragedy struck. Sherri died suddenly one morning, at home and at a young age. She was a strong Christian who loved her family and friends deeply, and she was my wife's best friend. We felt her family's loss as if we had suffered the loss of our own family member. It drew us, especially Kathy, closer to Sherri's children. I feel their pain even more now since Grayson was also called to heaven suddenly, at home and at a very young age.

Sherri was such a kindhearted person who had touched so many lives, and her funeral reflected that. It was the largest I had ever attended. It seemed like the entire town had come to pay their respects to her family and to celebrate her life. The service was beautiful and uplifting. Everyone talked about what a godly and giving person she was. She was a wonderful daughter, sister, wife, mother, and friend. We knew every good story and word of praise for her life was true. She was truly a special person.

All the stories told that day were positive—until John got up to speak. He decided he needed to say a few words. It was hard for him to keep his composure while talking about his mother, who had died just a few days earlier. It was very hard for him indeed, but what a blessing for all of us who listened to his words. What he said changed my family, and I am confident it changed many other families as well.

John spoke to us about the day his mother died. He'd had an argument with her that morning. There were words exchanged, and he left for school on a bad note. This type of morning between a teenage child and his mother is not unlike what most families experience from time to time. Every family with teenagers has mornings like this, probably more than we like to acknowledge. No big deal, except he would never be able to talk with his mother again. He would never get the opportunity to apologize to her. He could never tell her how sorry he was for speaking to her in anger or get to tell her one more time that he loved her so very deeply.

That is the story he told us while he fought back tears. I still find it unbelievable he had the ability to get through his story without totally breaking down. John's telling of this story was not only a message to his mother about his deep love for her, but it was also a message to everyone in attendance. John shared his painful story with us in an effort to help us avoid ever having to experience the same pain and anguish he was feeling that day. He shared this message with the huge crowd attending his mother's funeral. I have never been as proud of a young man as I was of John at that moment.

John told his story not for sympathy or forgiveness but to make everyone aware that this could happen to them. His message was to never leave a loved one in anger because you don't know when God might call them home. Most people never think when they leave a family member with unkind words that it could be the last time they see them. I know I never thought it could happen to me. But the emotion with which John told his story while fighting back tears made us all think about how we should talk to our loved ones every time we leave them. His desire was that no one hearing his story would ever find himself or herself in the same situation he was in. What a selfless message from a young man in immense pain.

After that day, every member of my family said "I love you" to each other numerous times daily. Whenever one of us left the house and whenever we finished a phone conversation or even a string of text messages, our closing remark was always "I love you." Grayson, being so close to John for so many years, was especially mindful to say these words. He didn't want the last thing he said to me, his mother, his brother, or his sister to be something in anger; he wanted it to be that he loved us. Do you understand how truly special that is? My twenty-six-year-old son told me he loved me at the end of every conversation and every time he left the house. Because of this young man's courage to tell his story at his mother's funeral, I know the last words I said to Grayson and his last words to me were "I love you." It is impossible for me to convey to you how much comfort and peace that knowledge continues to bring to me. It is something that I will cherish for the remainder of my life. My wife and children have the same comfort in knowing their last conversations with Grayson ended with a mutual exchange of "I love you."

After Grayson's death, I told John how much of an impact his story had on my life and on the lives of my family members. I told him that because of his story, each member of our family had eight years of expressing our love for each other and for Grayson up until the day he was called to be with God. And this practice has only been reinforced since Grayson's passing. As I have shared it with my extended family, it has become more meaningful to my family and a part of our conversations with each of our relatives as well. Talking or texting, we always finish with "I love you." That means so much when someone is taken away from you unexpectedly. I have no doubt God gave John the courage to speak at his mother's funeral so we could change our lives and now be able to reflect on so many words of love spoken between Grayson and ourselves. Priceless healing words of love.

I share this to encourage you to start expressing your love to your family members and close friends. It will strengthen your relationships and give you tremendous peace. It is good to do even if you never experience another loss in your lifetime. But, if you do endure another tragedy, it will give you the peace of knowing your final words were words of love. Please, talk with your family today about making this your practice as well. You will not regret it.

Thank you, John, from my entire family.

Chapter 6

Grieving Differently

❖

When you are dealing with loss, especially a loss that was sudden and unexpected, you must deal with grief. Grief will fill your days and nights for a long, long time. It has now been over a year since I lost Grayson, and I am still dealing with grief on a daily basis. I still cry nearly every day. My crying sessions are not as frequent, and they don't last as long as they did a few months ago, but the suffering relentlessly continues.

Everyone deals with loss and grief in their own distinct way. One way is no better or worse than another is. I don't think badly of anyone in my family if they don't grieve the way I do. I don't force my way of grieving onto my wife or children because my way may not be right for them. They need to deal with the loss of Grayson in their own ways—ways that help them to get through the pain that they are experiencing and get back to living their day-to-day lives.

Kathy and I share many similarities in how we deal with our loss. We read the Bible and books on grief daily, we talk with each other, and we pray together and with our family. We also work through our grief in very different ways, though. Her way helps her get through the day, and mine helps me. Neither of our ways are wrong. They are just different.

In the next few pages, I will share with you a few of the ways in which Kathy and I have had differing viewpoints and feelings related to our grief. Again, what I am attempting to show is that in dealing with grief, no one is right and no one is wrong. Everyone deals with loss differently, and whatever gives you peace is right for you, even if it has the exact opposite effect on others.

For many months after Grayson's death, Kathy did not want to leave the house because she would potentially see people she knew. Having people come up to her at the store or the bank would produce an overwhelming flood of emotions within her. These people always meant well and felt they must talk to her about her recent loss, but Kathy did not want to deal with these intense emotions on a daily basis. At least not at that point in her grieving process.

I completely understand her feelings on this point, but by contrast, after about six months of intense grieving, I was ready to go out and see people. I wanted to get the first awkward and emotional meetings over with and move forward. I felt I could go out and see people for the first time since the tragedy; I could talk with them, accept their condolences, and move on. I listened to what they said, processed it, thanked them, and continued with whatever I was doing. I found every well-meaning person who knew me would approach me and attempt to console me in public once. But after the initial meeting, the awkwardness and emotional conversations were over for the most part. The second time they saw me, they might ask how my family and I were doing, but other than that it seemed to be back to normal, with hand waves and talking about things other than my loss. To me, the quicker I got the initial meetings and condolences out of the way, the quicker I would get back to normal conversations and relationships with people.

I don't want to sound harsh or ungrateful. I appreciated hearing good stories about Grayson and seeing how people truly cared about him, but there came a point where I wanted things to get back as closely to normal as possible. My approach was to run as fast as I could toward that more normal place, even if it meant I needed to listen to a lot of nice people expressing their condolences on what seemed like a never-ending basis. Every first meeting was very emotional and usually had me tearing up and crying—crying to the point that I could no longer talk. These encounters drained me both physically and emotionally and were incredibly difficult to navigate my way through, but each was a major part of my healing process.

Kathy had no desire to work through her pain in this way. She needed more time to heal. She did not want the heartache of continually listening to condolences and reliving her loss, at least not this soon. My process of getting out in public and talking with people after six months or so worked best for me but was not right for Kathy. She needed more time to grieve in private and with her family.

One of Kathy's ways of coping with her grief is keeping a picture of Grayson as the background on her cell phone. She misses him so deeply that she wants his face everywhere. With his picture as her background, she can see his face every time her phone rings and every time she makes a call. Seeing Grayson's picture as often as she can has been a major part of her healing process. This practice started a day or two after Grayson was called home. It seemed like a natural thing for her to do.

Doing the same thing to my phone would just not work for me. I couldn't handle having Grayson's picture appear every time my phone rang, and I especially would not have been able to cope with it over the first few months. Whenever I saw a picture of Grayson in those early days, I broke down. Floods of emotions ran through my body every time I saw his face. I know I would not have been able to talk on the phone to anyone if my phone had been set up like Kathy's phone. What gave her peace sparked huge waves of sadness and anxiety within me.

Seeing Grayson's face multiple times each day as she used her phone was exactly what Kathy needed to ease her pain. It helped her so much to see a picture of her son throughout the day. It still does. I understood why she did this, and I thought it was great. I still do. I sometimes wished that I was able to do the same thing, but it was much too difficult for me. What worked for her and helped her cope with her sadness did not have the same effect on me.

Some of Grayson's loves were Oklahoma City Thunder basketball and any sport played by the University of Oklahoma. Grayson and I watched hundreds of Oklahoma City Thunder basketball games and OU football games together. A lot of our time together was spent talking about game results, recruiting, and player trades and predicting what was going to happen in the future. I have many great memories of these types of conversations and fun times that I spent with Grayson.

After his death, it became very hard for Kathy to watch these sporting events on television. She told me watching the first OU football game without Grayson was one of the hardest things for her to do. It tore her up inside because it reminded her that he was gone for good and would no longer be able to enjoy games with us. Even after that first game, watching the sporting events that Grayson loved without him continued to be so very painful for Kathy. I felt terrible when she told me because I had no idea it would have such an effect on her, that the games Grayson loved so much would cause her so much pain.

I, on the other hand, enjoyed watching these games knowing how much Grayson loved to watch them with me and talk to me about them. Whenever I watch games now, I think about how he would have reacted to whatever is transpiring. It makes me both happy and sad. I feel good and sometimes smile thinking about what Grayson would have said after every play or every possession (Grayson was not bashful about letting you know his opinions), but I also feel sad because he is not actually there saying those things to me.

It seems like almost every life event has both positive and negative connotations now. Good memories of Grayson definitely help me to heal, but the negative of no longer having him here to enjoy the events with me is a hurt that I will feel for the rest of my life. If the positive I receive outweighs the negative, though, I count it as a win. The good memories of watching sports with Grayson help me to heal more than the sadness of his not being there hurts me, and so it is a win. But again, in this case, what helps me deal with my pain and grief causes huge waves of sadness for Kathy.

After Grayson's death, Kathy and I started reading Christian books on loss and grief. We now have a library of books on this topic as well as podcasts and audiobooks on our phones that have helped tremendously to guide us through our grief. Reading was a huge part of our healing process. We often shared books to help each other deal with certain aspects of our loss.

Kathy still reads books every day. There is a lot of material out there on grieving and loss. You never know when a new book will present you with an epiphany, a perspective you had not thought of before. It seems Kathy finds a new book every few weeks, which is great. She continues to find healing in different authors' Bible-based viewpoints on loss. Reading Christian material has been and continues to be a huge part of Kathy's healing process.

I still read the Bible and daily devotionals and occasionally listen to podcasts, but I decided to begin journaling my thoughts and experiences (which led to my writing this book). At this point in my grieving, writing seems to give me the most comfort and helps me to gain perspective more than anything else I have tried. Writing down my feelings, my questions, and my desires brings me a little peace as I attempt to work my way through my grief. This is what works best for me now, while it is reading in which Kathy continues to find the most comfort and that is most beneficial for her.

There is one more difference I would like to share with you. It's not another example of different ways in which we grieve, but rather a very different way of viewing how time can heal pain. Throughout my entire grieving process, countless people told me that time would heal my pain. "It takes time," they would say, "for you to get over your loss and for you to heal." I probably would have said the same thing before I experienced the devastating death of my son.

What I believe to be true for me, however, is that I will never get over my loss and I will never stop hurting. I think over time I will get more used to the pain, and it may dull a little, but it will always be there. It's like the example I gave in chapter three of losing my arm. Over time, I will get used to the pain of not having an arm, but the pain of losing it will never go away. It will always be painful because there will always be something missing from my life. This may not be true for everyone experiencing a loss, but I would assume it is true for most.

So no, I don't believe that time heals our pain; it is our faith in God that provides the healing that we are searching for. Place your trust and faith in God and believe He will be with you while you are grieving. He will comfort you and give you peace in the midst of all your sorrow. Healing does not happen quickly, but with God's help, it will happen. Maybe instead of "Time will heal your pain" the saying should be "In time, God will ease your pain." That makes the most sense to me.

Remember, no one experiences loss in the exact same manner. Everyone has their own thought processes and their own ways of coping with life after a tragedy. Nobody can predict what will ease another's pain or what will inflict additional hurt upon them. Grieving is specific to each individual person; one size does not fit all. So be respectful of everyone's right to heal in their own way and your right to heal in your own way. You must find whatever helps you through your grieving and stick with it. Determining which activities help you make it through the day and which ones cause you more pain is very important. You will not get better or move forward with your life until you navigate your way through the grieving process. But remember, what works for you may not work for the rest of your family. Allow everyone space to work through the grieving pro-cess in their own way. Allow them to grieve in a manner that helps them to recover. Do not hinder their recovery by forcing your way of grieving onto them. There is no right or wrong way through this process, just your way and their way. Pray often and allow God to help you find what works best for you.

Chapter 7

Don't Listen

❖

I am writing this chapter to let you know that this time in your life, as you are experiencing tremendous pain and having trouble coping with all that is going on around you, is the time when the devil will begin to plant doubt and place terrible thoughts into your head. I am going to give you two examples of how this happened to me and how these horrible thoughts nearly crushed me. Satan may give you similar thoughts or thoughts even more debilitating. What I hope to show you is the need to recognize that the devil is real and that he is working against you. He wants you to suffer and be depressed. He does not want you to recover from this experience. He wants your life to be changed for the worse and for your relationships with God, your family members, and your friends to suffer. He will put terrible thoughts into your head. Don't listen! You need to acknowledge it is Satan putting these types of negative thoughts in your mind and pray to the Lord for comfort and direction. Pray for wisdom to recognize when the devil is trying to influence you and for strength to reject these terrible thoughts as they are put into your head.

The first example of the devil's placing doubt into my mind happened a month or so after the funeral. I was feeling numb to the world, and my depression seemed to be growing as I tried to process everything that had recently taken place and how my life without Grayson would be moving forward. I relentlessly questioned why this terrible tragedy had happened. My pain and heartache were overwhelming. Sadness filled my entire day, each and every day. I continually prayed for peace and comfort but felt like my prayers were not being heard, which only served to increase the level of sadness I was feeling. Why was God not answering my prayers? What was He waiting for? Why was there only silence?

One day, something or someone gave me a feeling of happiness—just for a brief moment. I don't recall exactly what caused this good feeling to come over me at that time. It may have been a story about Grayson someone told me or a memory of a happier time that popped into my head while looking at family pictures of Grayson. I don't know for sure, but I do remember feeling some momentary happiness. As I look back, I see that what happened next was surely the devil at work.

I experienced this happiness for a minute or less, and then a deep, deep sadness came over me. The thoughts now going through my mind made me feel terrible about myself. How could I feel happiness when I had just lost my son? I was disrespecting the memory of Grayson because I was not grieving his death in that moment. To respect his memory, I must continue to hurt and be sad. What a horrible father I was for having a moment of happiness in the midst of this terrible time in my life. Not just a horrible father, but a horrible person!

Thoughts like these quickly erased my moment of happiness and pulled me deeper into a depressed state. Over the next month, I experienced four or five additional moments of happiness, all ending abruptly with me hating myself even more for them. I was so ashamed of myself for having moments like these. It's hard for me to explain just how much damage these good feelings inflicted on my soul. What was wrong with me? Why was I having these flashes of happiness that ended up causing me even more pain and so much anxiety?

I agonized over this internally because I was too embarrassed to let anyone else know about these moments. It made no sense to me that I could feel any degree of happiness, no matter how minute, in the wake of my son's death. The terrible shame that I experienced had a crippling effect on me. I felt like I could no longer function in a normal manner. I felt powerless to stop the avalanche of horrible emotions that I experienced with every happy thought that came into my head. And still I wondered, why was I not receiving the peace that I had been continually praying for? Why were my prayers not being answered? Where was God while I was battling the immense pain that I experienced immediately after each moment of happiness?

Then God revealed something to me that completely changed my perception of these moments. What I am about to share with you helped me so much and will help you too if you are experiencing these types of dramatic swings in your emotions. It will cause the emotional roller coaster ride that you sometimes find yourself on to level out and become much more manageable. Are you ready? Here it is. The few moments of happiness I experienced were, in fact, the comfort from God I had been praying so desperately to receive. I just didn't realize they were the answers to my prayers because of all the negative thoughts the devil was overwhelming me with each time I received them. Only the devil could take something happy and turn it into something that hurt so deeply. God was answering my many prayers by giving me short moments of happiness in the midst of all my suffering. How great is that?

With this newfound awareness, I consciously made the decision that these moments were gifts from God and that it was okay for me to be happy. I allowed myself to cherish these moments rather than allowing them to make me ashamed and full of regret. And once I determined that it was okay to have moments when I was not grieving, it helped me to heal. It helped me so much.

Cherish the moments of happiness when they come. They are breaks from the pain that you so desperately need but may not realize you need. I am certain that these moments of peace, when I was not feeling completely devastated, came from God. He gave me a little happiness to help me cope with everything that was going on around me. I fought these gifts of happiness much of the time, believing that I should not feel good, even for a second. Once I accepted that it was okay not to feel completely overwhelmed by grief for a few moments, though, it was really healing. Those few precious moments helped me deal with all the pain I was enduring. It was so good to experience a few good feelings, even some joy, in the midst of all the suffering. They were exactly what I had been praying so hard to receive. I just did not recognize these periods of happiness as the answers God was providing to me.

I know it's hard, but when you make the decision to allow yourself to be happy, even for the briefest time, you will mentally be better for it. Being angry, depressed, confused, and everything else negative takes its toll on you. The negativity you feel drains you physically, emotionally, and spiritually. In order for you to receive the much-needed recharge, you need to allow yourself to have brief moments of happiness every now and then. The recharge God sends to you does not have its intended effect if offset by feelings of guilt. Don't allow the devil to steal these healing moments of joy God is providing to you. You need them so desperately.

The point I am trying to convey to you is that it is okay to have happy moments after your loss. Think about what I just said for a moment because I think it is extremely important for you to process that statement. Say it aloud and let it sink in. Say, "It is okay for me to have happy moments," and "They are gifts from God." You have to allow yourself to receive and be thankful for any small breaks from the anguish you are feeling. It's okay to quit crying and smile for a minute or two. You need this time so desperately. And when you do have these moments of joy, remember to thank God for providing them to you because they are definitely His easing of your pain.

I wish someone had shared this with me early in my grieving process. I foolishly allowed the devil to take some of God's precious gifts of happiness and distort them into something horrible for much too long. So much healing I could have experienced was lost because I listened to the devil's lies. When he lies to you, don't listen. Eagerly and thankfully, accept these happy moments of healing sent to you by God. You need them so very much.

My second example of the devil placing horrible thoughts into my head centers on my role as the head of my household. This position is one that I take pride in and cherish so much. The devil used my strong feelings toward leading my family to distort and confuse me. He chose to take something that means so much to me and use it to cause me additional pain.

I believe grief for the head of the household is different than it is for the rest of the family. As the head of the household, my job is to take care of my family, period. That is my one-line job description. It is a job I work hard at every day, trying to provide for my family and make sure they are happy, safe, and protected.

After Grayson's passing, I felt like a complete failure because I could not protect him from dying. This feeling of failure and despair hit me so very hard. I knew there was nothing I could have done to prevent this tragedy, but I still felt the guilt. I had not taken care of my son. I became severely depressed, overwhelmed by my self-destructive mindset, and did not know if I could go on. I know this was the devil at work. He kept whispering horrible thoughts into my head. He wanted me to continue the downward spiral I found myself in. He wanted to beat me down and damage my relationships with God and my family. He was making me a bitter person and trying to crush me with all the guilt and pain. He knew exactly where he could hurt me the most, and it was working.

I didn't know what to do but turn to God once again and pray for guidance. So, I prayed to God and asked Him to comfort me and guide me through this terrible situation I found myself in. And, after dealing with these horrible feelings for a few months, God turned my outlook on my loss completely around. All my doubts and dark thoughts began to fade away. I acknowledged that Grayson's death was not my fault. There was nothing I could have done to prevent his death. I had known that all along; I just needed the Lord to get rid of the negative thoughts the devil was continually placing in my head.

The Lord also showed me that while I was struggling with this doubt I was letting my family down by not taking care of them and their needs in the midst of their grieving. I needed to stop focusing on my own negative thoughts and start being a leader for my family. I prayed then, and continue to pray every day, for God to grant me the wisdom to help my family. It is not about me; it is about them. As the head of the household, I had to take this position so that I could lead my family through this terrible time in their lives.

If this sounds like your story, and if you are the head of your household, you must do the same as soon as you are able. Do not listen to the devil as he tries to put doubt and negative thoughts into your mind. Don't let him make this time in your life and the lives of your family members even harder than it already is. Don't let depression consume your life. You must be the rock and the comforter to your family. They need you now more than ever. Continually ask God for wisdom and guidance for you and for your family. He wants to help you; you just need to ask Him. He has helped me to lead my family through our loss and continues to help me daily. He will absolutely do the same for you.

What you are feeling is normal. With an accidental death, everyone close to you will potentially feel they could have done something to stop the tragedy from happening. Kathy and I struggled with this a lot. We thought there was something we could have done to prevent Grayson's death. This is a gut-wrenching feeling that can overwhelm you. These types of thoughts caused us immense pain and despair, but I firmly believe this was the devil at work trying to destroy the remainder of our lives. He was trying to break us to the point that we would no longer be able to function. And he did break us, at least partially, but fortunately for us, God fixes the broken. God continues to heal our brokenness, and He continues to care for us during this extremely difficult time in our lives.

The devil may attack you in the same manner that he came at me, or he may use completely different areas of your life to cause you heartache. Regardless, what I believe you can be expectant of is that he will attack the good in your life. He will take what you care about the most and use those strong feelings against you in an attempt to steal your remaining joy. Recognize that he wants to keep you down and separate you from God. Don't listen to his nonsense. Pray for the ability to recognize when the devil is placing these terrible thoughts into your head and ask for the capacity to reject them as they come.

The devil is a liar. Don't listen to him as he tries to keep you down and make your life even harder. Don't listen when he attempts to block all happiness from your life and replace it with suffering. Don't listen when he casts blame on you or on others when no blame exists. Consciously recognize that the devil is behind these types of thoughts, and then ask God for peace and guidance. He will give it to you, although in your pain it will sometimes be hard to recognize. Look for His comfort and remember that it is okay to have peaceful and happy moments when your sadness seems to briefly fade. You need these moments so desperately as you battle through this devastating time in your life. Don't let the devil take advantage of you in your moments of weakness. Be strong, be prayerful, and trust that God will heal your pain.

Chapter 8

Family Gets Even Closer

❖

M y family has always been close. It was very important to both Kathy and me to have our children close to extended family while they were growing up. When we needed a babysitter, we always had family available, and we made it a point to include our children on every vacation we would take. Today, all my children, my mother and father, my in-laws, my brother and his family, and my sister and her family all live within a thirty-minute drive. We all get together for Christmas, Thanksgiving, and birthdays. Spending time with family is a huge part of our lives. We have been very blessed to have always had family nearby.

We have always believed family is one of the most precious gifts God has given to us. We have treasured our family our entire lives, and Grayson was a huge part of our family, loved and cherished by all of us. He has a special place in each of our hearts. Losing him has been devastating not only to our immediate family, but to our entire extended family as well. Grayson was the first grandchild on both sides of the family, so his grandparents and his aunts and uncles were especially close to him. Their relationships were closer than most other extended family relationships that I have witnessed.

Even though Grayson's grandparents, aunts and uncles, and cousins are all missing him and dealing with the loss in their own way, I am going to address how I see the loss affecting the members of my immediate family and myself. I will first tell you how Grayson felt about each of us and then how I see losing him has affected each member of our family.

I will start with the youngest of our family, Caroline. Grayson always told his mother and me how much he loved Caroline. He said she was the most caring and thoughtful person he had ever known. "A lot of people do wonderful things for recognition," he would say, "but Caroline does those things because she is genuinely a good person." He loved and respected his little sister so much. While I was living out of state and Kathy would drive down to visit me, Caroline would often cook dinner for herself and Grayson so he could have some good home-cooked meals. That meant the world to him. I think that while I was working out of state it allowed Grayson to grow even closer to his sister.

Grayson would do anything to protect Caroline and keep her safe. After Grayson was called home, Caroline spoke at his funeral. Caroline said that she had lost her protector and that Grayson was now her guardian angel. She believes he continues to watch over her. She can feel it.

Caroline had an experience, the first of four, with Grayson after he was taken home. Grayson passed in his sleep, and Caroline found him the next morning.

Since she was the one who found him, the police needed information from her regarding what had happened. While she was answering questions about how she had found her brother, she became overwhelmed with grief and asked to be excused to go to the restroom. She walked out into the hallway and prayed to God for strength, and as she did, Grayson came to her and told her everything was okay and that he was in a good place. He gave her one of his usual lines, "It's all good." Caroline immediately experienced an over-whelming sense of peace come over her because she knew Grayson was in heaven. What an amazing feeling! With her new peaceful disposition, she went back and answered the questions that needed answering. Even after his death, Grayson was taking care of his sister.

Grayson had a very close and special relationship with his brother Austin as well. Austin was a husband and father by the time he was twenty-one. With a wife, a son, and two jobs, he still managed to attend college and obtain his degree. Grayson always said it was amazing Austin could graduate from college with all he had on his plate. Grayson would tell us he was proud of what a great husband and father Austin had become at such a young age. He was so proud of him for handling all his responsibilities and for being such a great man. He loved his brother very much and was in awe of his accomplishments. He made it a point to tell this to his mother and me often.

For about a year, Grayson lived with me out of state and would travel home with me on the week-ends. Nearly every weekend, he would tell his mother and me that he was going to drive up to the city to see his brother, and when he did, he would usually spend the night and sleep on Austin's couch. He wanted to spend as much time with his brother and his brother's family as he could. He became good friends with Austin's wife, Darian, and spent a lot of time getting to know Callum, his only nephew. Austin appreciated this and grew even closer to Grayson during this time. For a long time after Grayson's passing, Austin said it was strange to not be receiving a call from Grayson every Friday afternoon to ask if it was okay for him to come over and hang out. Austin misses those phone calls so very much.

Austin told me shortly after the funeral that he would often go out into his backyard, look up at the sky, and talk with his brother. He would tell Grayson what was going on in his life. This gave Austin some much-needed peace. Austin still talks to Grayson from time to time. In his car driving home from work or whenever the need arises, Austin keeps Grayson up to date on his life. His brother is still there with him in spirit.

Now for Kathy. Grayson would always tell me he absolutely, hands down had the best mother in the world. He could not imagine anyone having a better mother than he had. He loved and appreciated all she did for him more than he could ever possibly express. He would often say he couldn't believe how his mother had stood by his side and helped him through life. She often told him that he would always be her son and she would always be there for him, no matter what. Grayson knew this to be true. Grayson said he loved his mother so very much, and he made sure everyone knew how much he loved and appreciated her. He felt blessed to have Kathy as his mother.

Kathy was and continues to be devastated by Grayson's death. Like me, she could not make sense of why he was taken, and that made her extremely depressed. Part of her healing process was decorating our home with Bible verses that reminded her of Grayson. These verses, displayed prominently in our house, are there to bring comfort and hope to all who read them. They are also there, along with photos of Grayson, in part as reminders of him so that he will not be forgotten (of course, if you know Grayson, you know he is impossible to forget). Grayson will always be in our hearts, but these verses and pictures help to reinforce that fact. They allow us to think of him and actually see his face on a daily basis, which we all agree is awesome.

There is a bond between a mother and her child that I don't think I truly understood until now. Grayson loved his mother dearly, and Kathy loved him even more. Losing Grayson may have been the hardest on her. She suffers tremendously, and there seems to be nothing I can do to ease her pain. Her love for Grayson was a very strong bond between them. It still is. She misses him more than I can express in words. It is an unspeakable pain that she deals with daily. Every day I pray for God to bring her the peace she is so desperately searching for. She desperately needs God to heal her sorrow and bring some happiness back into her life. I know He will.

I guess it is my turn now. Grayson told me so many times I was a great father, friend, and role model for him. He often wrote this same phrase on birthday and Father's Day cards that he would give to me. Do you realize how amazing it is to have your son make these types of statements to you many times a year for several years? What a special young man it took to say and write those kind words to his father. Those words will stay with me for the rest of my life. I know Grayson loved me, and just as important, he respected me as a person. Knowing this gives me tremendous comfort as I continue to struggle with not having him around. I am so thankful that God allowed Grayson to express his feelings to me on so many occasions, and I am also thankful to God for giving me Grayson for twenty-six years. What an awesome gift he was.

Grayson and I were always close, but when we shared an apartment together for nearly a year while I was working out of state, we became even closer. Can you imagine sharing an apartment with your father when you were twenty-six years old? I know I sure can't. But Grayson did, and we became even better friends for it. We played ball together and talked about the future, and I was able to give him life lessons and advice whenever he had questions. Since we were both living and working away from home, we just had each other to talk with.

When Grayson was offered a great position with a company in our hometown in Oklahoma, he struggled with leaving me in Texas with no family. As excited as he was at receiving the opportunity that he had been praying for so desperately, he still worried about me. How awesome is that? He only accepted the job after I assured him I would be fine and that he should do what was best for his career.

Over the four years before his death, Grayson and I played golf together at our favorite course maybe a hundred times. That is four or five hours per round of sitting in a golf cart together and talking—talking about family, sports, or life in general. I am so thankful now for that time I had with him. My pastor once told me he was amazed at the amount of time we spent with each other. He said we had spent more time together in those last few years of Grayson's life than most fathers and sons spend in a lifetime. We had squeezed a lifetime together into a much shorter time period. When I think about it, I know he was right. I thank God for allowing me to spend a lifetime with Grayson before He called him home.

After Grayson's funeral, our family talked about him and about how much he loved each of us. (That is, in part, how I knew what to write in this chapter.) This helped us to grow even closer as a family. We have prayed as a family, gone to church as a family, and spent time together as a family more since the funeral than we ever did before.

Mutual love for Grayson has also brought us closer to other loved ones. Caroline's boyfriend, Tyler, has been a rock of faith for Caroline and for our entire family through this time. Darian, my son's wife, was always there for Austin during his grieving process. She was helping Austin even as she was grieving the loss of Grayson herself. My sister Staci, Kathy's sister Rita, and our niece Sarah were also there for Kathy, me, and the entire family. I could go on naming people. Everyone in our family ministered to us when we needed it the most. We found there are two things you need when you deal with a death: God and family. If you trust in God and keep your family close, you will be able to make your way through your grief and come out on the other side a changed person. You will be closer to God and your family from that point forward.

After our loss, our everyday lives changed in many ways. Obviously, most of the changes were very hard on us, but some were positive. Two changes of which I am the proudest came from Grayson's brother and sister. Austin calls his mother and me every day when he gets off work and often on his lunch break now. That is one of the biggest blessings to come out of this tragedy. We get to talk with Austin and hear about his day and his family. I am blessed with being able to discuss life and give him advice, much as I did with Grayson. Austin has told me he used to think being a man meant going out on your own and taking care of your business. He now believes being a man means being close to your family and taking care of them, making sure they are doing well. And he has taken this responsibility to heart. He is a great husband, father, brother, and son.

Caroline is in college and lives in a sorority house. Since Grayson's passing, she spends much more time at home and tries to sleep at our house as often as she can. I cannot express how much comfort and joy this gives to Kathy and me. Caroline's spending time with us is what we needed most while going through this life-changing event. She recognized this and made it a priority to be at home with us. What an amazing thing for her to do for her struggling parents.

Both of our kids have taken on the added responsibility of making sure Kathy and I are doing well, even while they continue to struggle themselves. What amazing children we have, and what a blessing they continue to be to us. I cannot imagine having better children. I love them both so very much. I know many people my age who see their children a couple of times a year. Kathy and I see Austin and Caroline multiple times a week and talk to them nearly every day. Like the title of this chapter implies, we were a close family before, but through this tragedy, our family has become even closer. This is truly a blessing from God for which we are infinitely thankful.

Banding together after Grayson's death was a natural response for my family, but I am sure that this does not happen to all families when they experience a tragedy. I want to encourage you to get close to God first and then focus on keeping your family together during this hard time. I have said this before, but if you don't turn to God first and receive peace and understanding for yourself, you will not be able to effectively lead your family through this difficult time in their lives. If your family was not close before the tragedy, this is the time to draw them back in and to become a close family again, or perhaps for the first time. If your family is close, as in my case, it is time to draw even closer and to be there for each other both now and in the future. You will need your family, as I need mine, for the rest of your life. I pray that you will find peace and your family will come out of your particular tragedy stronger and closer to God.

Chapter 9

Gifts from God

❖

B ecause it is so personal to my family and me, I struggled with sharing this chapter with you. But I needed to write it so I would always remember to thank God for allowing the events I am about to share with you to happen to my family. Whether you are a believer or not, what I am about to reveal to you can only be described as miracles or gifts from God. Once I tell you about the four amazing gifts that my family received, I feel you will agree with that conclusion.

This is my first experience with the unexpected loss of a loved one, so I really don't know if these gifts are normal or miracles only a few receive. I can tell you from the bottom of my heart, though, that they have meant more to my family and me than I can possibly express on paper. Words are not adequate to explain to you how much comfort they have given us and how they have helped us in our grieving process. They have also given us tremendous hope for the future because we know Grayson is doing well and is in a very good place. We know our Savior is watching over him.

Keep in mind, this chapter is specific to my family. You cannot necessarily expect to have the same experiences within your family. It is possible, however, that you could have your own special sightings of your loved one or completely different gifts from God. You just have to be on the lookout for them and cherish them if they happen. Look for your signs of hope and peace. If you find them, hold them close to your heart and know the one you lost is with our Savior and is being allowed to give you a sign that everything is fine and that you should not be worried about them.

Within six months after Grayson's death, God utilized Grayson to reveal certain messages to his family. I believe that God used Grayson to deliver His messages because He knew it would be exactly what our family needed. In our current state of hopelessness and depression from losing Grayson, we so desperately needed to see Grayson's face or hear his voice once again. God knew this and allowed Grayson to deliver His messages of hope. We received these signs or gifts from God on four separate occasions. Each sign, witnessed by a different member of our family, was unique in its delivery and conveyed a distinct message to us. Each message gave us a measure of peace in the present and unbelievable hope for the future. Each was a miracle from God lessening our grief. What incredible gifts for us to receive!

As I tell you my story about receiving these four gifts from God, please keep in mind that it was God utilizing Grayson to send his family messages of hope. So whenever I state that Grayson did something, know that I am actually talking about God. Also, much like how the Bible recorded Jesus speaking in parables, God's messages to us were also in story form. I will tell you what each of God's messages meant to me, but it may deliver a slightly or completely different message to you.

The first gift from God you read about in the preceding chapter. Grayson appeared to his sister Caroline shortly after his death. He confirmed to her that he was okay and told her not to be scared. He said, "I'm fine," and "It's all good." This gave her tremendous peace when she was really struggling. A sense of calmness came over her, and she knew her brother was in the loving arms of our heavenly Father. God allowed Grayson to take care of his sister and help her in her time of need. I can't think of anything else He could have done that would have had the same calming effect on her. Hearing Grayson say that he was in a good place was exactly what Caroline needed as she struggled with the loss of her brother. God knew this and sent him to give her the peace she so desperately needed.

This first gift or sign to our family showed us all that Grayson was happy and in a much better place. It came on the very day Grayson's earthly body died. God wasted no time in letting us know that Grayson was in heaven and that he was doing well. I have no doubt He did this to help everyone struggling with Grayson's death to be happy for him rather than sad that he had died and to help us deal with the horrible pain of losing him. I know in my heart Grayson and all my children will spend eternity in heaven; God used Grayson to confirm this for us on the very day he died. What an incredible gift.

Over the next few weeks, we shared this story with friends and relatives to give them peace too. A few words from Grayson to his sister made such a difference in so many people's lives. It was incredible how much comfort and healing that story gave to everyone who was suffering. I still smile when I recall my daughter telling me the story for the first time. On the worst day of my life, she told me that Grayson had come to her and told her he was in a good place. Wow! What a blessing from God! He allowed Grayson to give us all wonderful news in the throes of our nightmare. What a tremendous gift for us to receive.

The second gift from God came to me in my time of need. No doubt God could see how much I was struggling the first few days after Grayson's death, and He gave me peace in a very different way—in a way that was special and specific to Grayson and me.

As I said before, Grayson and I played golf at our favorite course a hundred times or more. It was a special place for us that gave us many special memories. In the days between Grayson's being called home and his funeral, I had numerous moments when I felt like I was about to experience a nervous breakdown. I was sad, stressed, and depressed. I was hurting so much that my body constantly felt numb and my mind was always in a state of confusion. I didn't know how or if I was going to make it through life without one of my children. However, over those few days, God sent Grayson to ease my pain and to provide me some much-needed comfort and peace.

Every time I began to hit a low spot, feeling exceedingly depressed about losing him, whatever I was thinking about would completely leave my mind. It would be replaced with an image of Grayson and me playing golf on that familiar course. Each time this scene played through in exactly the same way. I would be sitting in our golf cart, and Grayson would hit his ball, then sit down beside me and say something. I could never hear what he was saying, but he would always look at me, say something, and then give me his silly laugh and grin.

This great memory of Grayson only came to me when I was thinking about something extremely depressing and was becoming overwhelmed with grief. I would say the same scenario played out about fifteen times in total. The last ten or so times it made me smile and even laugh. I went from a breakdown to laughing. I don't know how to convey to you how much this helped me in my time of need. What a miracle it truly was. I saw my son at our favorite spot and got to see him laugh with me a few more times. It was a tremendous "Grayson gift" sent to me from God. Many months later, I considered that maybe God had allowed Grayson to have this same good memory come to him in paradise. How awesome would that be?

God's third gift to us happened a few months later. My sister Staci called me and said she wanted to tell me something about Grayson but didn't want it to upset me. She knew Kathy and I were still grieving immensely and struggling to get better. Thankfully, she caught me at a time when I was not crying and could actually hold a conversation with her. I told her I wanted to hear anything she could tell me about Grayson. I not only wanted to hear her story about Grayson, but I needed to hear it.

Staci proceeded to tell me that she had awakened in the middle of the night the previous night. Awake but groggy, she saw our grandfather who had died when we were children. We called him Papa. She had not thought of Papa in probably forty years, and neither had I. She said she saw Papa and still recognized him after all these years. He was walking on something that looked like a cloud. What she told me next was incredible. She said she then saw Grayson walk over and meet his great-grandfather for the first time ever. She said they shook hands and talked for a few minutes. Then they both reared back and laughed so hard their bodies shook.

Both my grandfather and Grayson loved life and had huge laughs, so it seemed natural to me that they would get along great and would have some spectacular laughs between them. Staci thought it was strange because, as I said, she had not thought of Papa in a very long time. Why would she see him now? She is convinced Grayson was walking around in paradise meeting people, some for the first time, and in doing so came across his great-grandfather who had died thirty-plus years before he was born. I believe God was letting us know that our family will all be reunited in the future. We will all be together in paradise for eternity. He knew my family was struggling with losing Grayson, and He was telling us not to worry because we will all be back together soon enough. He was attempting to ease our struggles once again by showing us that Grayson is well and in a very good place.

So to rehash, Grayson appeared and spoke to his sister, giving her comfort in her time of need and letting her know that he is in a good place. He took away my crippling thoughts and replaced them with great memories. And he appeared to my sister and sent a message to us that one day we will all be reunited in paradise. Pretty amazing, right? But wait until I tell you about God's final gift to us. It will absolutely blow your mind!

A few months after Staci saw Grayson and Papa, we received our fourth gift from God. Grayson appeared to his cousin Steven. At the time, Steven was a freshman at the University of Oklahoma. He was in the Pride of Oklahoma marching band and living in a university dorm room. One night, a week or so after Thanksgiving, Grayson came to Steven's dorm room and spoke to him. Steven said he could see and hear Grayson just as if he were physically in the room with him. They talked for several minutes. Grayson walked over to him and told him not to get out of bed. He told him that he was very proud Steven had made the Pride and happy he was doing so well in school.

As if this were not incredible enough, Grayson talked next about our family's getting together the previous week for Thanksgiving. He told Steven he had heard us reminiscing about past Thanksgivings. The specific Thanksgiving Grayson had heard our family members talking about was one several years earlier at my sister's house. Grayson had accidentally fallen into the swimming pool and gotten soaked. When this story was told, everyone remembered and laughed. Grayson said he had heard this story being retold and heard family members laughing at his predicament, but he made a point to say it was okay this story had been brought up. He said it was a very funny story, a good one to remember.

Steven had been growing a mustache, so Grayson then told Steven, "You are really rocking the stache." If you knew Grayson, you know those would definitely be his words of choice. Steven said they talked for a while, and then Grayson left. He later regretted not immediately sitting down and writing out everything Grayson had said. What I have written down is all Steven could recall of his talk with him.

I don't know why God picked Steven for Grayson to appear to and talk with. Selfishly I wish He had picked me. But, it is so special to know Grayson had a lengthy conversation with his cousin. It is also good to know that God allowed Grayson to watch over his family for months after he was called home. He must have been watching over us. How else would he have known what had been discussed a week or so earlier at Thanksgiving? My belief is talking to Steven about his mustache and his college experience was not the main purpose of his appearing to Steven. Grayson was getting the message to us that he is still a part of our family and, more importantly, that he hears us. What a great message to give to us at a time when we were overwhelmed with grief. I still feel that Grayson hears me whenever I talk to him. I thank God for being a caring and compassionate God who would allow me this peace. I also thank Him so much for the four incredible gifts He gave to my family.

I believe that God used Grayson as a messenger to comfort us and to communicate His wonderful messages to us as we continued to struggle with our loss. Who better than Grayson to deliver these four messages of hope to our family? Thank you, God, for allowing Grayson to show his family that You are watching over us, that You want to diminish our hurting, that one day we will be reunited with Grayson in paradise, and that he hears us. Much more importantly, thank You for letting us know he is with You and that "It's all good."

Chapter 10

You Will Be Changed

When you experience the loss of a loved one, it will change you. I have seen it happen to my family and to others close to me. There is no way to make it through such a traumatic event and avoid being changed. The question is, will your life be changed for the better or worse? I don't mean to imply you will have a better life without your loved one. What I mean is you can decide to be a better person, have a closer relationship with God, and help those God puts in your life, or you can be a depressed and reclusive shell of your former self. It's up to you.

If, in the midst of your suffering, you can summon enough strength to trust in God and truly believe that this horrific event was a part of His plan, you will be changed for the better. Your faith will be stronger, and your trust in our Savior will be unwavering. You will be better equipped to help those whom God puts in your path, and you will feel blessed. The unbearable pain that you are experiencing will begin to fade because of your faith that God is in control and the acceptance that your loss is a part of a much bigger plan that you can't comprehend. Trusting in God and having faith in Him to get you and your family through this horrible time in your life is the only way to survive your loss. This trust will help you to come through this tragedy a stronger and more committed Christian. That is what we should all be praying for as we battle through our pain.

As I touched on earlier, many people respond to loss by turning to drugs and alcohol rather than dealing with the pain. Drugs and alcohol have a way of masking the pain; they keep you from feeling it for a brief time. This is definitely the easier path to take. It is easier to continue to dull the pain you are experiencing than to deal with your loss. The problem with the easier path, though, is that with it there is no healing, there is no hope for the future, and your pain is constantly with you. Drugs and alcohol do not help you work through your pain. When you sober up or are no longer feeling the effects of the drugs, the pain is still there. So, you must either turn to drugs and alcohol again or at last deal with your pain. It is a vicious cycle many people find themselves in.

You may not care in your moments of profound grief, but having your family see you drunk or high will make the situation much worse for them. They will not only have to deal with the loss they are experiencing but also with a family member who is behaving recklessly. This will be just another burden for them to bear. Instead of helping them through their grieving process, you will give them even more grief to deal with. I urge each of you to think of others and how you can help them deal with their loss rather than turning to a substance to dull the pain you are experiencing. My focus has been on my family and helping them get through this painful time in their lives. Your focus should be on your family too. They need you now more than ever.

Both for your family and yourself, turn to God and ask Him for the ability to lead and care for your family and to keep your faith strong and unwavering as you lean on Him for guidance. Drop down to your knees and pray for these gifts you so desperately need. Once you receive them, you will be a changed person. You will be a positive example to your family and be better equipped to help them work through their pain and sorrow.

Experiencing a tragic loss tests everything we believe in as Christians. It tests our faith and changes our relationships with God, for better or worse. As I stated in an earlier chapter, it is during the low times of our lives that we have the opportunity to get closer to God and allow Him to heal our broken hearts. Drawing closer to God and allowing Him to comfort and guide you through your grief, accepting this gift He is ready to give you, is one of the greatest things you can do for yourself. I say this because I have experienced it and know it to be true.

I talk with God many times every day. This is the single most important thing I do to help myself make it through the day and to continue to lessen my grief and sorrow. I continually ask God for peace for my family and myself. I ask Him to give me the strength and the wisdom to help my family through this terrible time in their lives, and I ask Him to make me a man my family, including Grayson, will continue to be proud of. I am also mindful to thank Him for all He has done for me. I thank Him for my wife, who is amazing. I thank him for my son and daughter, who have blessed me and helped me more than they know. I thank Him for my entire family and for those close to us who continue to reach out to us, comfort us, and pray for us. I thank Him for continuing to watch over Grayson until our family is reunited sometime in the future. And I thank Him for getting me through the past few months as I have continually struggled with feelings of hopelessness and depression.

I have a much stronger and closer relationship with God now than I did before losing Grayson. I hope everyone who knows me will see that this tragedy did not beat me but made me a much stronger Christian. That goes for my entire family as well. We are stronger as a family unit, and we are each stronger in our faith. Although we still feel the pain of our loss, and probably will for the remainder of our lives, we have kept our faith strong and allowed this tragedy to strengthen us as Christians. That is one type of life change that I hope all who experience loss will undergo.

I pray the change in your relationship with God will be you drawing closer to Him and you trusting that this tragedy is part of His plan. Once this happens, you will feel the difference. You will experience the peace that you have been praying so hard to receive, and you will feel a great deal of comfort and relief as your healing begins.

When we experience a loss in life, I believe this gives us an opportunity to help others. Kathy and I have discussed on many occasions how, having gone through our loss, we are now better equipped to help others who are facing similar circumstances. Our loss has given us a depth of understanding we did not have before. We must now use this knowledge to help others who are experiencing losses of their own make it through the grieving process and come out stronger.

I know I am much better prepared to help someone handle the loss of a loved one and move toward healing than I was before I walked that road myself. The pain I have experienced gives me an understanding of the issues and potential pitfalls related to grief that most do not possess. That makes it my responsibility to help all those God puts in my life who are grieving in a similar way. I believe He will put people in my life who will need comfort and help that only those who have experienced a loss of their own can provide. My suffering has made me more sensitive to the pain others experience, and as a more empathetic person, I will be better able to provide the support that those who are hurting from a loss really need. I believe this is a good God has created from my tragedy. God has created this, but for it to truly have a positive effect on someone, I must step up and be the person God intends for me to be. Only through my actions will the good God created be manifested into a positive influence on a grieving soul. We must all do the same, should the opportunities arise.

I continue to be amazed at how God has helped my family and me make it through the absolute worst time in our lives and how He has caused it to change us for the better. He has taken something that caused each of us so much pain and so much heartache and used that experience to change our lives in a positive way. He has shown us that we need to be the light that shines through the darkness of our loss and that our story is not over—it is still being written. God will continue to take away our pain and when the story of our loss is completed, it will include God doing many great things through us. I truly believe that God will use every member of my family to help others in need of comfort as He places hurting souls into our lives. Incredible blessings will come from our loss. I have no doubt this will happen.

How will your loss change you? It is your choice. Will you allow God to help you emerge from your tragedy a better, stronger person, or will you come out a beaten, depressed, and bitter person? I pray the former for you. Let everyone see this did not beat you. It cannot and will not beat you if you ask for God's help. God does not want to see you in pain. Ask Him for peace, and you will receive it. Ask Him for guidance and wisdom, and He will provide it. He did for me. And always, thank Him for the many blessings He has given to you.

Chapter 11

Concluding Thoughts

This is the end of my story—the story of the most horrific experience of my life, the loss of my first-born child. It is an unimaginable and agonizing loss that I will bear for the remainder of my life. Yet my hope is that when you read this story of my loss, you read about victory and not defeat. I hope you see what an amazing God I love and, more importantly, that my God loves me endlessly and wants to ease my pain.

Originally, I felt extremely unqualified to write this book, having never written before. I didn't want to give someone bad advice that could potentially do more harm than good. But, this is truly a God thing. God not only put this book on my heart, but He kept pushing me to publish it. As I said in the introduction, God uses people who are hurting to bring a message of hope to those in need. I feel I have completed the task that God challenged me with, and I hope that I was able to convey to you what an incredible God we worship. He is the God who provides comfort and peace to us in our times of struggle. He is the God who destroyed death for us so that we could one day live together in paradise for eternity. He is the God who loves us all so very much.

I want you to realize there was no way I could have written this book in the state of suffering I found myself in over those first months. I was grieving incessantly and bearing an inconceivable hurt as I typed out each and every word. I hope you understand it was God who took my heartache and turned it into a message of hope.

Evidence of this is in how relatively easy the writing process was for me. I wrote the entire book over the course of a few months. In the beginning, I thought I was going to journal some of my thoughts. When I told Kathy I was going to start journaling, she gave me a very nice leather-bound journal in which to begin my writing. But, to my surprise, instead of journaling, I felt led to go directly to my computer to write this book.

The process was amazing. Whenever I felt led, I would go to my computer, say a short prayer asking God to guide me in my writing, and then begin to write. I would write a chapter at a time without giving it much thought. I wrote without drafts, talking points, or any other forethought. The words just came to me. I would sit down and type out an entire chapter at a time. A few days or several weeks might pass in between sessions, but whenever I felt led to write, I would go through the same routine and type out another chapter. Truly, God was directing my thoughts and using me to write out my story. I was the vessel through which He wrote this book. I know that sounds like something you would read in the Bible, but it is the undeniable truth.

The supernatural ease I experienced with writing this book went away once the manuscript was complete.

At that time, the full impact of my grief returned, and I found it difficult to read the printed draft. I printed out the manuscript intending to proofread it for technical errors but found myself reading each chapter as if for the first time. It was bizarre and amazing all at once. The first time I tried to read it through, I couldn't read more than a chapter or two before I teared up and became too emotional to continue. And every time since has been the same. Even now, as I sit here writing these final remarks, I have still not been able to read the entire book in one sitting. A flood of emotions overcomes me every time I attempt to read it. I have a feeling this may never change no matter how many times I try.

It is extremely difficult for me to share the story of my loss with you, but I am so grateful that God directed me to write this book. I am grateful for many different reasons, but there are three reasons that stand out. First and foremost, I am grateful that in some small way this book may help someone who is dealing with a loss understand some of the emotions they are feeling and realize that what they are feeling is normal. I hope I can convince them, and convince you, that more than anything, the Lord is what all of us who are grieving need to get through this pain. As I said earlier, it is almost impossible to get through a loss in your life without God by your side. You need Him so much right now.

Second, I am grateful I will have this book to give to my family. We will have it to remind us of the signs God allowed Grayson to bring us and the incredible messages we received from each sign and to memorialize how God gave our family peace in the present and hope for the future at a time when we desperately needed both. This book will also help us to remember how our amazing God brought us out of the depths of our pain and sorrow when we thought we would never again experience joy in our lives. My family will always miss Grayson. This book will help us remember all the good and loving times we had with him while he was alive by showing us how much he still loves us even since being called home.

Finally, I am grateful because I actually feel how excited Grayson is about this book. I know it makes him extremely happy it was written to help those suffering through a loss. Grayson was always willing to comfort those in need, which is why I know how very excited he is about the potential for healing to come from this book. He will be watching to see the good that comes from reading the words God directed to be written. I may never know if this book gives anyone the peace I hope it will, but Grayson will know. He will be watching for the gain to come from our loss. I know whenever someone receives comfort from anything written in this book, Grayson will be smiling down from heaven. Smiling because he is genuinely happy for each and every person who receives some peace. Grayson has a very kind and loving spirit that I believe will live on through the reading of this book.

I pray reading this book has brought you some perspective on the gamut of emotions you are feeling—perspective from someone who has lived through a tragic loss of his own. My hope is that you have read this book with an open heart and have found some peace for your soul. If this book has, in fact, brought some measure of peace to you through your grieving process, the tears that went into it will have been worth it. Helping those struggling from loss is the reason God directed me to publish and share my story rather than keeping my feelings private and only sharing my journey and experiences with my family. My hope is that reading about the loss I experienced will help you and others in similar circumstances make it through all the pain and grief that you are currently feeling and emerge stronger and more committed Christians. I pray the reading of this book helps you deal with your loss by leaning on God for comfort and direction. It is the only way to make it through such a horrible time in your life.

I don't want you to think reading this book, or any book, will take away all your pain. It won't. Dealing with the loss of a loved one is the single hardest life-changing event anyone can ever deal with. I continue to cry nearly every day because I miss Grayson so very much. That will probably not change for the rest of my life. My hope, though, is that I conveyed to you the peace God wants for you and how you can receive that peace. I hope I conveyed to you what God has done for my family and me as we traveled through the lowest, most depressing time in our lives. He has given us strength, wisdom, comfort, and purpose as we continue our individual walks with Him. I pray He does the same for you.

What follows this chapter is an afterword. This afterword was included to provide you with several Bible verses full of comfort, hope, and the promises of God. These verses are very important to me. They gave me peace and comfort as I struggled with the loss of my son. I believe they will be treasures to you as well, as you work your way through your own healing process.

While this book is about my story, my perspective on my loss, and the hope that I received from God, the afterword is about *you*. It is about you moving forward. It's about you finding your peace, your hope, and the love God has for you through His Word.

I don't want to stop any emotions you might be feeling right now, though. Read the afterword at another time when you are less emotional—at a time when you are ready to dive into the scriptures for guidance and comfort. For now, take a deep breath and take a few minutes to reflect on what you have read. Think about the different chapters of the book and the effect they may have had on you. Are there one or more chapters you felt spoke strongly to you or related more to your current struggles? Say a short prayer and see if there is something God puts on your heart to read again. And if there is, please go back and read it one more time before moving on to the afterword. I believe God will reveal something to you that you truly need, if you listen to Him.

You need God now more than you can possibly know. Do not turn away from Him, but turn to Him. He wants to take away your pain and sorrow. Keep your faith strong and rely on Him to comfort you and to guide you through the remainder of your life. Be strong both for yourself and for your family. Always remember with God by your side, you are never alone and you are always loved.

Afterword

◈

A few months after I finished writing this book and was finally able to read through it entirely (but still over a period of a few days), I noticed the lack of Bible verses throughout. This seemed odd to me because reading the Bible helped me so much during my struggles, but I feel I wrote my story as God directed me to write. Maybe the point was to keep the flow of my story moving forward without stops to look up passages in the Bible. I don't know for certain, but I believe verses relating to this topic will truly be helpful to you, so I have chosen to include them here. I hope these verses minister to you, reveal to you God's promises, and help you as you continue to heal from your loss.

◈

To begin, I specifically want to share with you two verses that helped me early in my struggles and continue to help me as I move forward. These two verses have meant so much to my family that we have memorialized them in different ways.

The first verse that I want to share with you is a verse that Caroline painted on a canvas and gave to Grayson as encouragement to continue to work hard toward his goals. That canvas is now in the living room at our lake house. This verse is also inscribed on Grayson's headstone. It is Deuteronomy 31:6, which reads, "Be strong and courageous do not fear or be in dread of them, for it is the LORD your God who goes with you. He will not leave you or forsake you" (ESV). This verse shows that we serve a God who will never abandon us, no matter what we do or how we act. No matter what obstacles we face, God will always be right there with us. Grayson hung this verse by his bathroom mirror as a daily reminder—a reminder for him to be courageous as he worked toward his future plans. He loved this verse and loved even more that his sister had painted it for him.

The second verse is Romans 8:28: "And we know that all things work together for good to them that love God, to them who are called according to his purpose" (KJV). Recall that I mentioned earlier in the book that we have Bible verses prominently displayed in our house. This is one of those verses. This verse gives me confidence that there is a reason for my loss, even though I have no idea what the reason is. I have faith that God has a plan, and He will use my loss for good in this world.

The following are additional verses that continue to help me and I pray will help you as you work your way through your loss. They reflect God's promises of comfort and hope.

Blessed be the God and Father of our Lord Jesus Christ, the Father of mercies and God of all comfort, who comforts us in all our affliction, so that we will be able to comfort those who are in any affliction with the comfort with which we ourselves are comforted by God. (2 Corinthians 1:3–4 ESV)

"Blessed are those who mourn, for they shall be comforted." (Matthew 5:4 ESV)

He heals the brokenhearted
And binds up their wounds. (Psalm 147:3 ESV)

"Do not fear, for I am with you;
Do not anxiously look about you, for I am your God.
I will strengthen you, surely I will help you,
Surely I will uphold you with My righteous right hand." (Isaiah 41:10)

These things I have spoken to you, so that in Me you may have peace. In the world you have tribulation, but take courage; I have overcome the world. (John 16:33)

And my God will supply all your needs according to His riches in glory in Christ Jesus. (Philippians 4:19)

The LORD is near to the brokenhearted
And saves those who are crushed in spirit. (Psalm 34:18)

God is our refuge and strength,
A very present help in trouble. (Psalm 46:1)

Therefore, since we have a great high priest who has passed through the heavens, Jesus the Son of God, let us hold fast our confession. For we do not have a high priest who cannot sympathize with our weaknesses, but One who has been tempted in all things as we are, yet without sin. Therefore, let us draw near with confidence to the throne of grace, so that we may receive mercy and find grace to help in time of need. (Hebrews 4:14–16)

For I am convinced that neither death, nor life, nor angels, nor principalities, nor things present, nor things to come, nor powers, nor height, nor depth, nor any other created thing, will be able to separate us from the love of God, which is in Christ Jesus our Lord. (Romans 8:38–39)

"Come unto Me, all who are weary and heavy-laden, and I will give you rest. Take My yoke upon you and learn from Me, for I am gentle and humble in heart and YOU WILL FIND REST FOR YOUR SOULS." (Matthew 11:28–29)

"For I know the plans that I have for you," declares the LORD, "plans for welfare and not for calamity to give you a future and a hope." (Jeremiah 29:11)

For I consider that the sufferings of this present time are not worthy to be compared with the glory that is to be revealed to us. (Romans 8:18)

Even though I walk through the valley of the shadow of death,
I fear not evil, for You are with me;
Your rod and Your staff, they comfort me.
You prepare a table before me in the presence of my enemies;
You have anointed my head with oil;
My cup overflows.
Surely goodness and loving kindness will follow me all the days of my life,
And I will dwell in the house of the Lord forever. (Psalm 23:4–6)

"Do not let your heart be troubled; believe in God, believe also in Me. In My Father's house are many dwelling places; if it were not so, I would have told you; for I go to prepare a place for you. If I go and prepare a place for you, I will come again and receive you to Myself, that where I am, there you may be also." (John 14:1–3)

Rejoicing in hope, persevering in tribulation, devoted to prayer. (Romans 12:12)

"The thief comes only to steal and kill and destroy; I came that they may have life, and have it abundantly." (John 10:10)

Jesus said unto her, "I am the resurrection, and the life: he who believes in me will live even if he dies, and everyone who lives and believes in Me will never die." (John 11:25–26)

"Truly, truly, I say to you, he who believes has eternal life." (John 6:47)

Therefore there is now no condemnation for those who are in Christ Jesus. (Romans 8:1)

For His anger is but for a moment,
His favor is for a lifetime;
Weeping may last for the night,
But a shout of joy comes in the morning.
(Psalm 30:5)

"Very truly I tell you, you will weep and mourn while the world rejoices. You will grieve, but your grief will turn to joy." (John 16:20 NIV)

"So with you: Now is your time of grief, but I will see you again and you will rejoice, and no one will take away your joy." (John 16:22 NIV)

I want to leave you with two final verses. There is one verse that gives me hope above all others. This verse is well-known and sums up our hope for the future in a short, twenty-five-word sentence. God paid the ultimate price by sending Jesus to die for us and give us everlasting life. Can hope for the future be set out any better than that? This verse is John 3:16:

> "For God so loved the world that He gave His only begotten Son, that whoever believes in Him shall not perish, but have eternal life." (NKJV)

My final verse of comfort and the verse that I want to end with comes from the book of Revelation. It is a promise that the way things work in life now (death, etc.) and the consequences of that (grief, etc.) will all be things of the past. Think about that promise for a minute. It is difficult to comprehend just how great eternity will be for us. It will be such a different life than the one we now know—no more death and no more pain or grief. What a great promise God has made to us! This verse, Revelation 21:4, gives us all the comfort of knowing that these things will pass and we will only experience goodness and joy throughout eternity. In your time of grief, I hope it gives you as much comfort and hope for the future as it has me. It reads:

> And He will wipe away every tear from their eyes; and there will no longer be any death; there will no longer be any mourning or crying, or pain; the first things have passed away.

I pray that these verses will prove helpful to you as you continue your journey through your loss. They definitely help me and give me comfort and direction as I continue to work through my pain.

May God bless you and your family. May He give you hope and comfort in your time of sorrow. And, may He give you the peace you so desperately need as you struggle through life without someone you love so dearly.

Grayson,

I love you and miss you so very much. It still seems unreal to me that you are gone. The pain and heartache that I have experienced is unimaginable and still overwhelms me at times. Without you in my life, it has been extremely difficult for me to make it through each day. My everyday life became so much sadder and so very different because you are no longer here with me. It's hard for me to express how much I truly miss seeing you and talking with you every day. I would give anything to talk with you just one more time, to hear your laugh or see your silly grin. You will always be my son, and my love for you will never fade. I just needed to tell you that one last time.

Thank God for giving me comfort in knowing that you are with Him in paradise. I have thanked Him so many times, but you can deliver the message to Him in person! How awesome is that? Knowing where you are and who is looking out for you has made moving forward with life a little easier for me, mom, Austin and Caroline. We all still miss you so very much, but we have the comfort of knowing that one day we will all be with you in paradise for eternity. I am so looking forward to seeing you smile and hearing you laugh once more.

Love always,
Dad

CPSIA information can be obtained
at www.ICGtesting.com
Printed in the USA
LVHW012001020320
648718LV00006B/849